Shades of Meaning

Shades of Meaning

Reflections on the Use, Misuse, and Abuse of English

Samuel R. Levin

WestviewPress
A Division of HarperCollins*Publishers*

Copyright © 1998 by Westview Press, A Division of HarperCollins Publishers, Inc.

Published in 1998 in the United States of America by Westview Press, 5500 Central Avenue, Boulder, Colorado 80301-2877, and in the United Kingdom by Westview Press, 12 Hid's Copse Road, Cumnor Hill, Oxford OX2 9JJ

Library of Congress Cataloging-in-Publication Data
Levin, Samuel R.
    Shades of meaning : reflections on the use, misuse, and abuse of
English / Samuel R. Levin.
        p.   cm.
    Includes index.
    ISBN 0-8133-9028-1
    1. English language—Synonyms and antonyms.   2. English language—
Jargon.   3. English language—Syntax.   4. English language—Usage.
I. Title.
PE1460.L43   1998
428.1—dc21   97-48286
                                                          CIP

10   9   8   7   6   5   4   3   2   1

TO MY WIFE

Contents

Introduction

As NATURAL SELECTION WOULD HAVE IT, the human mouth is used in both eating and speaking. And just as in eating there are rules of proper etiquette, which tell us how to eat, so in speaking there are rules of proper usage, which tell us how to speak. Among the rules for proper eating, two of the most important are "Use the right fork and don't eat too much." In close correspondence, two of the most important rules for proper speaking are "Use the right word and don't talk too much." I am not sure to what extent present-day eaters observe the rules of etiquette just mentioned. It is an obvious and sad fact about current discourse, however, that a good many speakers fail to observe the corresponding rules of proper usage: Imprecise word choice and verbal excess are all too common in contemporary speech. This book, therefore, has two primary purposes: The first is to bring together pairs of words whose meanings overlap and to indicate the basis for their respective uses; the second is to identify and discourage the use of certain expressions that comprise a surplus of verbiage.

Insistence on use of the right word is, however, not simply a matter of linguistic etiquette. Words have meanings, and meanings have consequences: They project impressions of a person's mental state, and they define relations between speakers and conditions in the world. And if the distinctions among meanings are not observed, the state so described or the relation so defined may be quite different from the one intended. More than semantic nicety is involved, therefore, in choosing the proper word. If a person uses *disinterested* when intending to convey the lack of interest, a segment of personal experience is misrepresented. In similar fash-

1

ion, misrepresentation is the consequence if *rebuke* is used when a reproof is intended, if *entailment* is used to describe mere involvement, if *impracticality* is used to describe impracticability, if *satiation* is used when mere satisfaction is involved, if the word *elemental* is used instead of *elementary*. These few examples represent a mere sampling from the hundreds of comparable cases that are discussed in the following pages. A good part of this book is devoted to developing an awareness of semantic nuances in order to encourage semantic scrupling in the use of one's language.

There is still another sense in which the word chosen should be the right word. We require not simply that the word be precise but that it reflect good lexical manners as well. Violation of this latter requirement produces expressions that are not simply imprecise; they project also an impression of bad linguistic taste. Consider the remark made by a participant in a contemporary domestic argument: "This discussion is not about anything substantive; it simply bespeaks of our respective egos." Or consider the case where an announcer, after describing conditions in Port au Prince as turbulent, said that elsewhere in Haiti the situation was "becalmed." Or consider the use of *simplistic* in the following sentence: "I have a simplistic plan that will solve all your problems"; or the sign recently posted outside a courthouse that asked for "Equanimity under the Law." What we have in such examples is not simply a use of the wrong word but a lexical affront, an outrage upon our sense of semantic fitness. Errors of this particular variety do not so much call into question the speaker's knowledge of the language as raise the question of what might possibly motivate them, and the answer turns out frequently to be an overweening (although unsupported) desire to sound linguistically sophisticated.

Frequently going hand in hand with this penchant for lexical extravagance is a predilection for syntactic inflation. Those speakers who transgress the stricture against lexical impropriety also usually violate the stricture against verbal surfeit. This dual pattern of abuse, when sustained, produces a variety of language characterized by a swollen and pointless diction. By way of individual examples, consider the following two sentences—one illustrating syntactic, the other lexical, excess: (1) "It is up to the governor to make a determination about (instead of simply *to determine*) the most efficient way to raise revenues" and (2) "I have found Alka Seltzer to be an effective remediation (instead of *remedy*) for heartburn."

Overspeak and Its Manifestations

In the following section I consider various usages, some in the area of syntax and some in the area of word meaning. Among other things, the comments that I will make in the area of syntax are intended to point up, and perhaps serve to reverse, a drift in the language toward a condition that I will refer to as "overspeaking," a tendency to use, of two possible modes of expression, the one that comprises more words, that thus lasts longer, and that, in consequence, keeps the speaker for a longer time holding the floor. This tendency, although most marked in the deployment of syntactic units has, with some speakers, a counterpart in the manner in which they select individual lexical items, where the excess takes the form not of additional words but of additional syllables. Motivating both types of departure from the norm seems to be the idea that extra time spent in speaking is, *as such*, a linguistic good. The fact is, however, that substitutions motivated by nothing more than a wish to speak "long" usually compromise and undercut the ability to speak well. A rule worth remembering is that what is shorter said is generally better said.

Always, in the practice of overspeakers there is the striving for more "airing," more exposure, the greater presentation of self. This effort may manifest itself in the span of a single word or in the stretch of an entire speech. To begin with the domain of words: Instead of *single, singular* will be used; instead of *method, methodology;* instead of *motive, motivation;* instead of *definitely, definitively*. But these replacements do not simply win time for the speaker; they alter, in most cases significantly, the intended meaning. This fact, however, if at all appreciated, is overridden by the passion for speaking time. To the speaker, these exchanges, in which sense is sacrificed for duration, represent worthwhile trades.

The effort among overspeakers is to use the language so as to make what they say more needful of attention, not, to be sure, by reflection on the substance of discourse—the matter being discussed—but by the maximal use of "attention stretchers," words or expressions that require extra processing. Thus, instead of "I think that (the economy will improve)," we get "I suspect that (the economy will improve)"; instead of "He should look at this bill and see whether it should be passed or not," we get "He should look at this bill in terms of whether it should be passed or not"; instead of "I hope that (we'll see you at the party next week)," we get "I'm hopeful that (we'll see you at the party next week)"; instead of "A large contribution was made by Mr. Sloan," we get "A large contribution was made on the part of Mr. Sloan." Another factor is also at play in these usages. The phrase "I think that," for example, is colorless, the routine way to express the meaning in question; "I suspect that," in being a deautomatized (foregrounded) use, calls attention to itself and casts a refracted attention on its user. The same effect is produced by the other examples. This element of implied or suggested self-importance is another characteristic of "overspeak." Consider also in this connection the usually vacuous use of "clearly," with which some speakers introduce their response to a question—a response whose content is typically commonplace and that does little or nothing to clarify the issue under discussion.

People seem to be avid for speaking time; we see this reflected in the practice of politicians, those who speak for the education establishment, psychological counselors, and experts of various kinds, all of whom are eager for print and television exposure and who, when afforded the opportunity to express their views, seem determined to make the most of it. Television personalities, as well, are not inoculated against this tendency. Among the latter, it is a common practice when interviewing an expert in some field to follow a question with an exhaustive survey of all the possible answers. Thus, instead of simply asking "What in your opinion should the administration do to stimulate the economy" and waiting for an answer, the commentator will add the subsidiary questions: "Should the Federal Reserve Board lower interest rates, should the Congress revoke the capital gains tax, should the administration enact a series of public works programs, should . . . ?" I have heard an economist, on being asked a question of this nature, respond, "After the way you put the question, I could just as well leave now." Lawyers make the point that when a question is asked, and all its possible answers spelled out, the questioner has put a bad question, in that it allows respondents to "pick" the component of the question that they are willing to respond to, a component that may be tangential to the fundamental issue. Practicing economy in the asking of questions, however, militates against the craving for "air" time and so must give way. It is very refreshing when a speaker makes a point or asks a question, then *stops*—and does not dribble on (as I just have).

Perhaps nowhere is this tendency to be "present," to command the stage, more strikingly in evidence than among the participants in various talk shows. On some of these shows, we frequently witness what amounts to a speaking frenzy, a verbal contest wherein each participant struggles for maximum presentation before the viewing audience. It is really embarrassing sometimes to see grown men and women contend—with raised voices and strained countenances—for a five- or ten-second extension of their speaking time. "I have more to say, don't cut me off," they seem to be saying. Moderators of these programs have their hands full trying to allot time equitably, this problem assuming existential dimensions when the moderators themselves are engaged in the struggle. One such specimen is so intent on exercising the proprietorial right to "air" his own views that no sooner has one of the assembled experts begun to answer one of the moderator's elaborately formulated and lengthily put questions than the moderator interrupts the answer to his own question and proceeds to answer it himself. In this way he manages to maximize his speaking time and, incidentally, himself: His face dominates the screen and, what is more important, his voice monopolizes the air.

With some speakers the need to speak amounts almost to a lust. This species, once in possession of the floor, will never willingly relinquish it. On being asked for their contribution to the topic under discussion, they proceed to spin out sentence after sentence, with no thought of stopping. Speakers of this sort are not so much articulate as they are verbally facile; their mouths seem to be set on automatic pilot. With such speakers the floor passes to another only when their flow of verbiage is forcibly interrupted. In order to effect its purpose, moreover, the interruption must be sustained. The result—an awkward period of cross-talking wherein both speakers struggle for possession of the air—is a public embarrassment.

Turn to a congressional hearing sometime. You will witness one of our elected officials in speechifying action. At times, it appears that the principle of highest resort does not at all relate to the matter at hand, that is, to the legislative or parliamentary issue under discussion. By no means. The principle of highest resort, it soon becomes apparent, is speaking time. It is common to hear a senator or representative speak for fifteen or twenty minutes and make, belabor, and remake a point whose gist would provide sustenance for two or three simple sentences. And there seems to be a correlation between this verbal edema and the use of speeches to make political rather than substantive points. Moreover, when politicians in the furtherance of such a point wane philosophical, they expect attention to be paid. I have heard someone in the well of the House wind on for twenty minutes to an empty chamber and enter, in the midst of a diatribe against the opposite party, a complaint to the covering network against its practice of panning the empty seats, a practice that the speaker found demeaning. "I am speaking," the speaker seemed to suggest, "and significance must be assumed."

There is a difference between speaking and saying. It is possible to speak without saying anything. In its ultimate form, this would be accomplished by uttering nonsense syllables. Should someone speaking English suddenly produce the phonetic sequence "risdrilop avurmonu," nothing would be said thereby. But nonsense can be produced by other means than that of uttering nonsense syllables. Any speech that does not make clear its intent or advance the point at issue can be regarded as nonsense. Like racing the motor with the gears in neutral, speech that is simply vocalization, the mere activation of vocal cords, speech that does not add sense to the discourse, is *non*-sense; words are spoken but nothing is *said*. "He spoke for over an hour." "Yes, but did he say anything?" Unfortunately, this question is becoming increasingly more pertinent in our linguistic universe. In fact, considering the inverse proportion that frequently obtains between the extension of speech and the accession of substance, it would not be amiss to propose as a new adverb for the language the form *furtherless*.

The impulse to push the language beyond its customary limits represents a natural and defensible human inclination. And frequently these "creative" forays into the language's outer semantic precincts have happy outcomes. Consider, in fact, this last phrase. Can an outcome really be happy? This phrase can serve as a paradigm for an entire class of expressions in which an adjective originally used to describe a human feeling or attitude is juxtaposed with a word that refers to something altogether different—compare "joyful announcement," "jealous look," "angry reply," "enthusiastic support," and countless others. The semantic change involved in such cases is subtle, since it involves not so much the meaning of the word whose distribution has been extended as our conception of those things that are now modified by the words in their extended ranges. In other words, to answer the question just posed, there is a sense in which an outcome—this abstract, insensate affair—can indeed be happy.

In the preceding development we have a good example of how a language undergoes change. We may assume that, at a certain time, for whatever reason, it occurred to a speaker to transfer one of the attitude-describing adjectives into an unprecedented context—the result being, say, the phrase "happy outcome." This novel juxtaposition was then responded to favorably by other speakers, the principle it incorporated seeming well motivated and its consequences deemed to fall within the implicit limits of the language's expressive potential; the newly coined phrase thus became a *model* for similar extensions and, with time, English possessed a new usage. In general, the process works in the following way: With the coming to adulthood of the innovating speakers, those speakers transmit the new usage to their children. When the children in their turn reach adulthood, the innovatory construction is at home in the language, passive resistance to it having passed away along with the generation of older, *non*-innovating speakers.

Not all linguistic innovations are like those described in the preceding paragraph, innovations, that is, that have behind them a "creative" impulse and are at the same time well founded. Some innovations result simply from an insecure grasp of the language's proper scope and efficacy, so that "creative" as they may be, their disregard of the language's inherent structure and capabilities disqualifies them from acceptance. Other innovations result from the misbegotten desire of certain speakers to sound linguistically "advanced": Such speakers, by using unexpected (and unwarranted) forms, confer on their speech a specious kind of verbal grandiosity.

Junk Language

When something presents itself as a form of commodity but lacks the substance or fails in the function commonly associated with that commodity, we call it junk. Thus, we call food junk when it fails to provide the known benefits of wholesome, nutritional food. We call bonds junk when they fail to afford the solid collateral backing that sound, high-quality bonds customarily afford. Similarly, we call mail junk when it fails to contain information relevant to our practical concerns or correspondence of personal interest. When, now, we find a set of expressions that lack linguistic substance and serve no communicative function playing a role in our language, we cannot but notice how similar is the linguistic form of dysfunctionalism to the types of functional degeneracy presented here earlier. Purely on the basis of analogy, therefore, we would seem to be justified in referring to expressions that are functionally otiose also as junk—that is, we might, on a par with speaking of junk food, junk bonds, and junk mail, speak also of **junk language**. The following paragraphs comment on some egregious instances of the linguistic junk that may be observed in current usage.

Consider the conjunctive expression *if in fact*. One proper use of this phrase requires the prior mention of some development or other. In the following examples, this requirement is met: A man tells his wife that he has stopped gambling, to which reported development she replies, "If in fact you have stopped (or "If you in fact have stopped"), then our marriage has a chance." Or someone says, in response to the time-honored temporization, "If in fact your check is in the mail, then the deal might go through." In such cases, the addition of *in fact* confers upon the replies a tinge of skepticism or dubiety, a calling into question of the reporter's trustworthiness, alludes perhaps to the sorry fate of previous such promises. In other words, the added *in fact* performs a communicative function.

The phrase is also used in connection with the antecedent mention of an as yet unrealized contingency; thus: "Many experts predict a downturn in the economy. If in fact this prediction is borne out, then the Federal Reserve may have to lower interest rates" (or "If this prediction is in fact borne out, then . . . "). In contrast, to reply when someone asks whether you are coming to a pending meeting by saying "I'll come if in fact my schedule permits it"; or to inform a friend that "I'll have this novel completed by early fall if in fact my work schedule holds" would introduce totally unmotivated uses of the phrase. In such sentences, the *in fact*'s, having no logical role to play, stand out as syntactic clutter (your interlocutor is not interested in responding to the uncertainties in your life that such responses vaguely imply). Such uses thus raise the question of what motivates them, and the dismal answer, which holds in general for the use of linguistic junk, is that the speakers entertain the misguided belief that the additional verbiage adds an impressive dimension to their use of language.

A somewhat related case is represented by *the fact of the matter*, an example of language bloat that is particularly favored by politicians and petty officials. In most cases where this phrase is used, *the fact* is all that is required—more important, is all that is correct. The full phrase is properly used when one of the participants in a discussion decides that some of the comments have been aimless or irrelevant, at which point—to focus the discussion on what ought to be regarded as the central issue—the participant may say (for example), "The fact of the matter is that taxes have not yet been properly adjusted"; in such cases, *of the matter* serves to downgrade and set aside the relevance that other aspects of the problem have been made to assume in the preceding discussion. But use of the full phrase without such a background of various and perhaps conflicting aspects in a discussion is simply an exercise in self-indulgence, an exercise that leaves in its wake a litter of linguistic junk. Yet how frequently are we required to listen through repeated and totally vacuous occurrences of that lifeless excrescence *of the matter*. The insidious spread of this verbal trash is brought home by a use like the following: "You may protest all you like about the cost of travel, but the fact of the matter remains that costs in the past five years have not matched the rate of inflation." In such utterances, "the fact remains," a compact and idiomatic usage, has been arbitrarily and clumsily dismembered.

Another locus of junk is the phrase *point in time*. More and more these days one hears expressions like the following: "At that point in time there was a lot of activity in the precinct," "We're all out of Beaujolais at this point in time," "I'm sorry but I'm unable to talk to you at this point in time." The following sentence was perpetrated by an economist: "Prices are coming down, but at the same point in time demand remains weak." In the latter example, the phrase *point in time* is revealed as having become syntactically frozen, as being considered, implicitly, to constitute a single unit—in fact, that the word *time* no longer performs a function by itself but counts only as part of a single morphological body, allowing of no decomposition, much like such words as *notwithstanding, moreover,* and *nevertheless*. The important point, however, is that in the phrase "at this (that) point in time" the demonstrative pronoun already specifies a particular time—a point in time, if you will—making the use of *point* in the phrase completely superfluous (alternatively, it may be understood as referring to the particular point to which events have progressed, thus making the reference to time unnecessary; cf. "At that point, the discussion became heated.").

As one more example of this junkward drift, there is the phrase *whether or not*. In its basic function, *whether* introduces a disjunction between two alternatives. Consider (1) "Kaitha couldn't decide whether to watch TV or read the newspaper." In a sentence like (1), where two disjuncts ("watch TV" and "read the newspaper") are explicitly mentioned, addition of *or not* would be superfluous and would serve only to complicate the sense of the sentence—by implicitly multiplying the number of relevant alternatives. But when the sentence contains only one alternative, then *or not* plays a role, as the negation of that alternative. It may play that role explicitly in the sentence, or it may be omitted and function implicitly, as in (2): "Gifford asked Francine whether she wanted to have dinner with him." The significant fact about constructions like (2) is that in the absence of a second disjunctive choice, the hearer tacitly supplies an *or not*. Francine could perfectly well have responded, "I'm sorry, Gif, but I'm busy tonight," responding thus to the implied negative disjunct. It is in constructions like that of (2) that abuse of the expression begins to occur, for example, in (3) "Gifford asked Francine whether or not she wanted to have dinner with him." In this sentence the segment *or not* could be added after *him*, but it has little or no business turning up attached to *whether;* it merely sets up a momentary and perverse intimation that Gifford put a question to Francine quite regardless of whether she wanted to have dinner with him (or not). Consider, further, such syntactical monstrosities as the following, which evolution of the usage has led to: "That fact has nothing to do with whether or not the prisoner is guilty or innocent"; or "When I awoke the following morning, I wasn't sure whether or not I had been dreaming or whether or not the events had actually happened to me"; or "This medicine is effective against any sickness, whether or not it is organic, whether or not it is functional, or whether or not it is psychosomatic."

Of some speakers we say that they speak French (or Spanish, say, or Japanese). Of those who liberally employ expressions like the ones just cited, we could say that they speak Junk. In fact, recalling George Orwell's Doublespeak, we might presume to define a new linguistic variety: **Junkspeak.** The general use of this variety contaminates meaning and stultifies common discourse.

The correlation that obtains between overspeaking and the use of junk language should be obvious. Junkspeak serves the speaker's need for more "airing." But this need is satisfied in a variety of ways, the examples discussed earlier representing merely one particularly striking variety, one in which the abuse—that of "holding forth"—is effected in the form of overdrawn syntactic formations. The same abuse is also manifested in the area of lexical selection. Thus, instead of *single, singular* will be used; instead of *method, methodology;* instead of *motive, motivation;* instead of *definitely, definitively;* instead of *signal, signalize* (recently, a speaker about to launch into a lecture on the virtues of a certain diet asked the members of his audience to "listen attentatively"). Such replacements do not simply win time for the speaker, however; they alter and obscure, in most cases significantly, the meaning the speaker intends.

With the advent of cell phones, beepers, answering machines, E-mail, and similar technological means of communication, another form of linguistic junk has entered the language. These devices obviously have their serious and substantive applications. More and more, however, in their employment, the language is being used not so much to communicate anything as it is to set up occasions when communication might take place; the function of language is reduced to a means for "keeping in touch." In conversations employing these instruments, the prevailing sign-off is not "good-bye" but "I'll get back to you." In other words, a communicative channel is established that is then used not to present information or discuss ideas but to say "let's communicate." Speakers using these instruments are not really exchanging views or information but are simply "presenting" themselves, so that although there is much more "communication" (we are flooded with messages), less than ever is being communicated. Like the type of linguistic junk described earlier, this variety also, in keeping speakers "longer on the scene," serves to project their presence and magnify their sense of self-importance. And how often is this self-magnification achieved at the expense of someone else's sense of personal dignity, as when, during a conversation or discussion of no matter how important, significant, or personal a nature, the phone rings, or the beeper beeps, and your conversation is interrupted—is "put on hold"—while your correspondent is summoned to address matters that may be of the most insignificant or trivial nature. And these summonses, of course, are peremptory; they must be obeyed.

The knowledge that we have of our language is essentially intuitive in nature; this means that although we may use the language with complete facility, we are unaware of the mental operations that we perform in doing so. When a speaker processes a complex sentence, a number of subtle and intricate calibrations take place in that speaker's mind. Such exercises are conducted at great speed and are essentially tacit in nature. Frequently, in order to shed light on whether a usage is good or bad, it is necessary to explore this "deep" intuitive level of linguistic consciousness. In dealing with the examples in this book, the emphasis is thus not entirely on whether they represent proper usage; a good deal of attention is paid also to the underlying grammatical and semantic considerations that determine such usage. More often than not, the analysis of these considerations throws an unexpected light on the question at issue.

Many of the articles that follow analyze slight differences in the meanings of certain pairs of words. Examples are pairs like *doubtful/dubious; eventually/ultimately; complex/complicated.* If these words are looked up in the standard dictionaries, it will usually be found that among the several senses given for each word there will be one sense that is the same for both. This makes it appear that the words are to some extent synonymous. But this apparent synonymy should not be overestimated. One should not thereby conclude that for all practical purposes it is a matter of indifference whether one uses one or the other of the two forms. The fact is that the difference in form—no matter how slight—usually signifies an original difference in meaning, a difference whose presence may still be discerned but which imprecise usage has first disregarded, then attenuated, and finally obscured. Thus, the lexicographical practice of listing the same sense among the definitions for the two words should not be regarded as offering a sanction for imprecise usage; it merely records what in the opinion of the editors is the state of current usage. In any event, the overriding consideration lies in the differences between senses, not in the similarities.

This brings us to another important point. Unlike those speakers whose use of the language is actuated by an effort to use it so as to enhance their personal image, there is another type of speaker who makes perhaps the same errors but not for the same reasons. It is not always easy to select the right word. Semantic gradations, as we have seen, are frequently quite refined. In many cases, therefore, errors—assuming that they are committed in good linguistic faith—may be caused by a simple lack of lexical discrimination. The remedy for this inadequacy, however, is not an unthinking adoption of those usages that are coined by linguistic "strivers" (it is this unwitting practice, in fact, that may account for the spread of these "nouveau" usages); the remedy is the same as that for an equivalent deficit in other fields—namely, study and application. There is no substitute for placing oneself in a position to experience excellent usage. The reading of good books is essential; when, in the process, a new word occurs, it should be looked up and its verbal nuance cemented into one's lexical register. Recourse to dictionaries, although not always decisive, is therefore an essential step— semantic pay dirt is frequently to be found there.

At times figuring in the analyses that follow—and throwing light on the problem at hand—is a discussion of the etymology or historical background of the items in question. Additionally, I treat in these pages various matters of grammar, syntax, and general usage, with here and there a problem or an aspect of language that momentarily took my fancy. It may be said of the grammatical and syntactic analyses that most of them bear significantly on questions of usage—the use of one form instead of another leading frequently to awkward, imprecise, or just plain incorrect use of language. A factor figuring in the background and playing a personal (one might even say a prejudicial) role in the selection of the usage entries is my personal impatience with locutions that result from speakers' trying to make themselves look good at the expense of the language, that is, by *ab*using the language, a dereliction that I regard as much more to be deplored than the simple *mis*using of it.

As a living language, English is in constant flux, with new forms and locutions continually pressing for admission. Some of these forms increase the expressive power of the language; they are, for that reason, to be welcomed into the linguistic fold. Others, as the preceding discussion has shown, merely increase the time that speakers take to express themselves, in the process frequently conveying an unintended sense or disguising the meaning altogether. Not all innovatory practices, therefore, have equally valid claims to universal acceptance, and it is up to us, as speakers of a language with a long and noble tradition, to regard as a matter of extreme seriousness our obligation to pass judgment on the merits of the various claimants. I believe that our obligation to pass judgment is even heavier when it involves usages whose motivation is open to suspicion. Finally, I should say that whatever crotchets appear here are my own, as are any errors, oversights, misjudgments, and failures of insight.

A Compendium
of Articles Dealing with
Questions of Meaning,
Grammar, and Usage

absolve/acquit: one is absolved of blame or of responsibility but is acquitted of a charge, usually a crime. The words are therefore correctly used in the following sentences: (1) "His wife absolved Jim of any blame that he might have felt over the loss of her credit cards; she claimed that it was her responsibility to look out for them" and (2) "Jane acquitted her husband of Mary's criticism that he talked too much." Compare also (3) "The judge absolved the defendant of guilt and acquitted him of the crime."

abysm/abyss: *abyss* is a rather straightforward development from a Greek etymon *abyssos*, meaning "without bottom," formed by adding the negative prefix *a-* to the word meaning "bottom"; the form *abysm*, however, derives ultimately from a Latin superlative form *abyssimus*, having the meaning "most deep." There is little to distinguish between the two forms, although knowledge of the fact that the meaning of *abysm* reduces etymologically to "most without a bottom" might lend it a bit more semantic weight; *abysm*, though somewhat the rarer of

the two forms, makes its presence felt in the adjectival form
abysmal.

(in) accord/accordance with: the use of one or the other of these
  forms is determined by whether what is being described is a
  quality or an activity. In use of the former, something *is* in accord with something else; in the latter, something *acts* in accordance with something else; compare "His conduct (a quality)
  was in accord with the school's regulations" and "He conducted himself (an activity) in accordance with the school's regulations." Exchange of *accord* and *accordance* in these two
  sentences would produce in each a lessening (rather than a "reduction") of precision.

achieve/accomplish: despite a considerable overlap in the meanings
  of these two words, it is possible to find in the respective ranges
  of their meanings a basis for distinguishing between their uses.
  Assume for *achieve* the meaning "to bring to a successful conclusion" and for *accomplish* the meaning "to perform fully." Common to both words is the meaning of something having been
  brought to completion; they differ in that the completion effected
  by achievement is more comprehensive, bringing to a close an extended process, whereas that effected by accomplishment may be
  isolated or constitute but a stage in a lengthier process. On the basis of these meanings, we may align objectives like success, happi-
  ness, and contentment with *achieve* and objects like jobs, purposes, and assignments with *accomplish*, where objectives are
  goals to be reached, objects tasks to be carried out. Consider the
  sentence (1) "Dick Yocum accomplished many worthwhile things
  in his short tenure in office, but he did not achieve the goals that
  he had set for himself." Interchange of our two verbs would
  slightly disturb the semantic equilibrium in this sentence. Compare now (2) "I finally got my son to clean his room—quite an
  accomplishment" and (3) "I finally got my son to clean his
  room—quite an achievement." It would be consistent with the
  meanings sketched here to read sentence (2) as meaning that it

was my son's cleaning of his room that was quite an accomplishment, but to read (3) as meaning that it was my getting my son to clean his room that was quite an achievement.

acquire/accrue: sentences like the following have been turning up in recent writing: (1) "The author enjoys noting the way fame is accrued in advertising," (2) "Smith has accrued a novel way of replying to his critics," and (3) "Reflecting on the use of mice in medical research, the author details the great benefits that science has accrued from this practice." In each of these sentences the word *accrue* is misused and should be replaced by *acquire* (or some equivalent). The meanings of these two words stand in something like an active-passive relationship. A person (or thing) is the subject of the acquiring process; a person (or thing) is the object or goal of the accruing process. Since *acquire* is an active verb, it may be rendered in the passive: thus, (4) "Peace of mind was finally acquired by Emily." But because of the intrinsic goal or object orientation of *accrue*, it may not be used in an active sense: thus, compare (5) "Emily finally accrued peace of mind." A bond, for example, may be acquired (i.e., a person may acquire it), but interest accrues to it; thus, it would be a mistake of the sort illustrated in (5) to say that the bond accrues interest.

action/activity: we say "At the time of this action," but "During the course of this activity." An action is punctual, an activity is durative; that is to say, an action takes place, an activity takes time. It is true that certain activities are at times referred to as actions; in relation to an artillery bombardment, for example, an officer might say, "While this action was going on, reinforcements arrived from the rear." In such cases, the activity in question has coalesced in the speaker's mind and is regarded as constituting a single atemporal exercise.

activate/actuate: when something is activated, it is made active, but when something is actuated, it is moved to take action (or produce a consequence). Thus, a person's sense of guilt might be activated by a look or a remark, but it would have been actuated by whatever it was that the person had done that produced the feeling of guilt in the first place. Compare (1) "Bill's remark activated Carson's sense of guilt" and (2) "It was his failure to have provided bonuses to his staff that actuated Carson's feeling of guilt." In (1) we assume that Carson felt guilty about something that had taken place and that Bill's remark reminded him of his guilt; in (2) we are told what it was that established Carson's feeling of guilt. In general, it would seem that something must be already present in order to be activated but not yet be in existence to be actuated.

acuity/acumen: both words refer to a keenness of mental powers. Their meanings differ, however, in that *acumen* suggests that this property relates to a person's mind, whereas *acuity* suggests that it relates to a person's performance; we might say that acumen is something that a person has, whereas acuity is something that a person displays. Acumen is therefore demonstrated generally, over a period of time, whereas acuity may be demonstrated from time to time, in specific applications. Acumen is attributed to a person on the basis of a record of performance, whereas someone can demonstrate acuity by a single penetrating observation.

addendum/addition: an addition is something that, when added, serves simply to augment or extend that to which it has been added, consisting in the same kind as and leaving unchanged the character of the original. By contrast, an addendum forms, when it is added, a separate, distinguishable portion of the whole. An addition to a book might be a few sentences interpolated here and there; it might even be a new chapter. But an addendum would be introduced as a supplement to an otherwise complete book (or other document). Thus, it might be a dedication, a foreword, or an epilogue. Supplements to clauses in a will would count as additions, but a codicil would be an addendum.

admission/admittance: both words refer to an entry (or entrance) into something or other; the difference, it turns out, depends on what that something or other happens to be. Consider the following sign observed outside an auditorium: "Admittance by pass only." Something seems wrong with this formulation. Suppose now that a brochure inviting membership in a club or organization includes the sentence "Admission to this club depends on a record of community service." Here again something would seem wrong. It appears that *admission* implies a physical entrance, whereas *admittance* implies some sort of procedural or merely formal entry. Admission correlates with permission to move into a room or building; admittance correlates with acceptance into a group or organization. Thus, with admission there is frequently associated a fee, with admittance the satisfaction of some requirement or other.

admit/concede: the relevant meaning of both words here is that of acknowledging something to be true. The major difference in their meanings is that with *admit* the acknowledgment applies to one's own sphere of conduct, whereas with *concede* the acknowledgment applies to another's. The contrast is strikingly illustrated in the following sentences: (1) "I admit my mistake" and (2) "I concede your point"; (3) "I admit that I was wrong" and (4) "I concede that you were right." Consider the inappropriateness of (5) "I admit that you were wrong" and (6) "I concede that I was right."

adventurous/adventuresome: both forms include the meaning element "prepared to enter into new and perhaps risky experiences." The significant difference between the two lies in the fact that whereas *adventurous* may be predicated of both a person and an undertaking, *adventuresome* is predicated only of a person. Therefore, we may have "Alan was an adventurous (adventuresome) person," but only "It was an adventurous expedition." *Adventurous* thus has as a secondary meaning: "comprising risk or danger." If we compare (1) "Alan was an adventurous explorer" and (2) "Alan was an adventuresome explorer," there is a suggestion in (1) that Alan was an explorer prepared to take risks, whereas in (2) the suggestion is that the expeditions undertaken by Alan were risky.

adverse/averse: *averse* is a predicate used of a person; a person is said to be averse to something, to something that is felt to be inimical to the sense of well-being; thus, a person might be averse to hard work, or to spinach, or to criticism. In daily life, that person will recoil from contact with these personal "aversions." Something is *adverse* to a person, however, if its impingement on that person would produce a negative impact on well-being. Accordingly, from the standpoint of a person, aversion is something that originates from within, whereas adversity is something that originates from without. A person is the subject of—feels—an aversion for something; a person is the object of—undergoes or suffers—an adversity. Where the nominal forms are concerned, it is not likely that anyone would confuse someone's aversion with adversity and use one of these nouns where the other was required. But confusion does sometimes arise in the use of the adjectives. Thus, faulty sentences of the following sort do occur: "Jason was not adverse to having dinner at the club," and "I'm not at all adverse to making a small contribution."

affect/effect: each of these two words has both a nominal and a verbal function. As a noun, *affect* means "a feeling or emotion," whereas *effect* means "the result or consequence of some action or process." As a verb, *to affect* means "to exert an influence upon," whereas *to effect* means "to bring about as a result." On the basis of their meanings, there is no great reason to confuse one of these words with the other. However, because of the similarity between them in both pronunciation and spelling, questions are sometimes raised as to their proper application. Primarily, this question arises in connection with the verbal function of these forms. Consider a sentence like "Whatever John does will not _____ the outcome that you desire." If *affect* is inserted in the slot, the resulting meaning is that nothing John does will in any way influence the desired outcome; but if *effect* is inserted, the meaning then is that nothing John does will produce or bring about the desired outcome.

aftermath: this word has an interesting etymology. In Old English the verb meaning "to mow" was *māwen, -en* being the infinitive ending. Associated with this verb was a noun *mǣth*, which meant "a cutting of the grass, a mowing," formed from the verb by addition of the suffix -th (cf. the similar formations *growth*, "the process of growing"; *health*, "the result of healing"; *ruth*, "the process of rueing"; and so forth). *Aftermath,* then, refers to the result of mowing, to the grass lying about after mowing. In the course of time the word has generalized its meaning to encompass a great many consequences other than those that follow upon mowing. In this process the homely echo of a farming activity is found to play in the semantic background of such sentences as "Tom and Doris found themselves curiously unsatisfied in the aftermath of their divorce" and "The storm left flooded basements, felled trees, and downed power lines in its aftermath."

amalgam/amalgamation: in general, an amalgam is what follows upon an amalgamation. An amalgamation is a process in which things are combined; an amalgam is the result or consequence of that process—a combination. In light of these distinctions, compare (1) "In Anthony Trollope's novels we find a happy amalgamation of keen social awareness and deep insight into the foibles of human nature" and (2) "Trollope's novels constitute a happy amalgam of keen social awareness and deep insight into the foibles of human nature." Exchange of our two words in these contexts would produce, it seems to me, a slight sense of semantic discomfort. In sentence (1), the intention is to highlight the process of combination that Trollope engaged in to produce the effect described; it reflects the fact that in reading Trollope, we keep being struck by how he distributes his efforts between the two dominant concerns. In sentence (2), the intention is to highlight the result, Trollope's achievement; it conveys the impression we have on finishing one of his novels, say, *The Warden*, of how successfully he has managed to combine the contributions of the two dominant concerns.

amend/emend: both words have the meaning "to improve, correct, or set right," but *emend* has this meaning in the specific area of textual revision; whereas one can *amend* various aspects of conduct or behavior, *emend* is used if the issue at hand is that of a manuscript, a speech, or literary product of any kind. Compare "Motz undertook to amend the defects in his debating style" and "Motz undertook to emend the syntactic irregularities in the text." An act of amending is an amendment, one of emending is an emendation. The form *mend* is a reduced—technically, an aphetic—form of *amend*.

amiable/amicable: these words are related in that both are borrowings in English, *amicable* from the Latin (*amicabilis*), and *amiable* from (Middle) French, in which language it was, at the time of the borrowing, the regular phonological development from the same Latin form. In Modern French, the form (having undergone additional phonological change) is now *aimable*. As to their meanings, both words mean "characterized by friendliness or goodwill." There is, however, a slight but significant difference in how that meaning is reflected in the two words. An amicable discussion, say, would be one in which the participants harbored a feeling of goodwill toward one another, whereas an amiable discussion would be one in which the participants *displayed* goodwill toward one another. *Amicable* implies the being well disposed, *amiable* the acting well disposed. Thus, in describing a person with whom one is acquainted, one would tend to use *amiable* rather than *amicable*, implying thereby that the speaker has personally experienced the other person's friendliness and good nature. Compare "I'm told he's an amicable fellow" and "I know him to be an amiable fellow." One would characterize an agreement or an arrangement as amicable, meaning that it had been amicably arrived at. These distinctions stem from, and are consistent with, the fact that *amiable* is oriented toward people—toward their actions and behavior—whereas *amicable* is oriented toward procedures that people engage in. A sentence like the following, recently encountered, should produce a somewhat skeptical reaction: "Given the sensitivity of the case, we tried for a long time to find an amiable solution to the flagrantly illegal proceedings." In one of his novels, William Thackeray refers on successive pages to an "amicable salutation" and an "amiable companion."

among/amongst: consider the following sentences: (1) "I pictured McFarland among the other distinguished intellectuals at the conference," (2) "I pictured McFarland amongst the other distinguished intellectuals at the conference," (3) "I rated McFarland among the ten leading intellectuals in the country," and (4) "I rated McFarland amongst the ten leading intellectuals in the country." Sentences (2) and (3) seem to use *among* and *amongst* properly, whereas sentences (1) and (4) raise some question. The difference appears to turn on whether or not (indeed!) the verb purports a sense of physical presence; when it does, as in (1) and (2), then *amongst* is motivated; when the verb does not purport such a sense, as in sentences (3) and (4), then *among* is motivated and *amongst* is contraindicated. Compare the following sentences, where the same factor appears to determine selection between the two words: (5) "I searched for the book among the biography titles" and (6) "I found the book amongst the biography titles"; further, (7) "They quarreled among themselves" and (8) "They distributed the profits amongst themselves."

-ance/-ancy: a fair number of nouns occur with both the suffixes *-ance* and *-ancy* (or *-ence* and *-ency*). Here is a partial list: *ascendance, ascendancy; dependence, dependency; resilience, resiliency; expedience, expediency.* The question is whether the slight difference in suffixation carries with it a difference in the meaning (or grammatical function) of the respective forms. To be sure, not all the relevant forms occur in pairs (cf., for example, *reluctance, redundancy, avoidance, remonstrance*). It appears, however, that where pairs do exist, a subtle difference in meaning in fact is associated with the difference in form. Thus, the following constructions appear to require one of the forms and exclude the other: (1) "Napoleon's ascendance to power was quick and total" and (2) "Napoleon's ascendancy astonished his fellow generals"; (3) "John's dependence on the goodwill of his coworkers was obvious" and (4) "John's dependency was obvious"; (5) "Mary's resilience in the face of her problems impressed everyone" and (6) "Jack's resiliency impressed everyone"; (7) "To escape blame, Jerry used the expedience of lying" and (8) "To escape blame, Jerry explored every expediency." Judging from the preceding pairs of sentences, selection of one or the other form appears to correlate with whether the noun is modified by a prepositional phrase (1, 3, 5, 7) and thus serves as the basis for a modifying relation or whether it occurs unmodified and functions of itself to describe a process or condition (2, 4, 6, 8). In the latter case, as the examples suggest, it probably follows a preceding use of the *-ance* form.

apparel/attire: both words refer to clothes, but a difference may be drawn between them concerning the manner in which each applies. Consider the following sentences: (1) "Edgar's apparel was obviously costly" and (2) "Edgar's attire was clearly stylish." In sentence (1), the predicate functions to describe the clothes that Edgar was wearing, whereas in (2), it functions to describe his manner of wearing them, so that *apparel* highlights the sense of clothes as material, *attire* the sense of clothes as dress. In line with this distinction, it would be appropriate, for example, to speak of "rich apparel" but of "tasteful attire"; of "loose-fitting apparel" but of "gasp-inducing attire."

approbation/approval: compare (1) "Basil expressed approbation of the plan" and (2) "Basil gave his approval to the plan." Exchanging our two words in these sentences would produce a slight sense of misfit in (2). The reason for this is that *approbation* in (1) suggests merely that Basil was satisfied with the plan—he approved *of* it, whereas *approval* in (2) conveys the more material sense that Basil *approved* the plan, that he accepted it. The effect of (2) is thus stronger, implying not merely the expression of approval but the granting or conferring of it—not merely praise or commendation for the plan, as in (1), but the actual sanctioning of it. Notice that one would say "Basil registered his approval of the plan."

arguably: a sentence adverb lately occurring with some frequency, as in: "Arguably, this proposal could save the city a lot of money"; "This plan is, arguably, the best one that has come before the committee." The word means, of course, "it might (or "it could") be argued that." Its relative novelty, or perhaps its whiff of logical rigor, have led some to an unreasoned enthusiasm for its exploitation; thus, a recent testimonial spoke of a new book as being "inarguably insightful." There is something mildly offensive about a formulation like this; it rules out, a priori and quite arbitrarily, any disagreement that a reader might have with the reviewer's aesthetic judgment.

argumentum ad hominem: translation: "argument directed at the man." When an argument takes this direction to divert attention from the facts relevant to the question at issue, it is regarded as a fallacious form of arguing. Consider the following case: Commissioner A proposes that his nephew be awarded the contract to build a new bridge connecting the boroughs of Manhattan and Staten Island. Commissioner B then declares, "My learned colleague (referring to Commissioner A) is recommending a person who has been evicted from his last three apartments for not paying his rent on time, and he expects us to take his proposal seriously." Instead of addressing the nephew's professional qualifications, Commissioner B directs his argument against the man, whose character is not the point at issue and whose record as a leaseholder has no bearing on the merits of the proposal. However, if Commissioner B's response were "My learned colleague is recommending to us a man whose previous three bridges collapsed within a period of three years, and he expects us to take his proposal seriously," the argument would not be fallacious, since the record of Commissioner A's nephew that is referred to is relevant to the question at issue.

ascribe/attribute: both words have the meaning "to credit, as to a source or cause," but the difference turns on whether what is being credited is of a concrete or an abstract nature. An anonymous letter that expressed resentment toward a critic, say, might be ascribed by that critic to a certain author (as its source), or it might be attributed to that author's dissatisfaction with a recent review (as its cause). It would therefore be appropriate for the critic to say either "I ascribe this letter to Meredith" or "I attribute this letter to Meredith's dissatisfaction with my review of his book."

as far as _____ is concerned: this is a discontinuous phrase, but it is a phrase, so that both segments are required for its proper constitution. Strictly speaking, therefore, a sentence like "As far as his fielding, that leaves nothing to be desired" has an uncompleted element and should be made to read "As far as his fielding goes (or "is concerned"), that leaves nothing to be desired."

as if/as though: these phrases are generally used interchangeably in clauses of comparison, but there appears to be a basis (an attenuated one, but worthy of remark withal) for distinguishing between them in certain contexts. In many cases it is a matter of indifference whether one says "It seems as if Bert does not approve of the new arrangement" or "It seems as though Bert does not approve of the new arrangement." However, under certain circumstances, particularly when the verb in the second clause is the substantive verb, a subtle distinction can be achieved by the use of one or the other of these two forms. Compare (1) "He spoke as if he was knowledgeable" and (2) "He spoke as though he were knowledgeable." Sentence (1) implies that the speaker in question was in fact knowledgeable, whereas (2) implies that he was not, that he merely gave that impression. The subtle point is that in these contexts "as if" conditions the expectation of the indicative mood of the verb in the second clause and thus that the condition described there is factual, whereas "as though" conditions the expectation of the subjunctive and that the condition described is contrary to fact. Compare also (3) "He acted as if he was sincere" and (4) "He acted as though he were sincere." The same distinction, it seems to me, may be derived from these, and similar, sentences. Consider further the following two sentences, which appeared in a recent review: (5) "The stories they tell are relentlessly uplifting; in fact, you begin to feel as if you're watching the climactic scene of a hundred television docudramas," and, shortly following, (6) "It's as if just by participating in this involuntary familial relationship . . . you are involved in a heroic political act." The "as if" in (6) is proper; (5) would be better rendered with "as though."

assay/essay: in their verbal function, both these words have meanings clustering around the notions of attempting, trying, testing, and the like. The difference between their meanings may perhaps best be appreciated by a comparison of their use in several sentences. Thus, compare (1) "He assayed his chances of success," "He assayed the quality of the workmanship," and "He assayed how much paint would still be required" and (2) "He essayed a minor criticism," "He essayed one more plea for leniency," and "He essayed to complete the bookshelf in three days." The meaning conveyed by *assay* in the sentences of (1) is that of testing in the sense of weighing, evaluating, and judging of; that conveyed by *essay* in the sentences of (2) is that of testing in the sense of attempting, venturing, and making trial of. The meaning of *assay* in these and other sentences in which it might occur is consistent with and perhaps derivative of the meaning it has when it is used in the testing of substances to determine their gold or silver content; in assaying an ore, for example, the assayer is testing that ore in order to assign to it a value.

attraction: in many syntactic contexts we find that the verb does not necessarily agree in number with the subject; compare the following sentences: (1) "The generation of computers now coming to market is superior by far to those that preceded it" and (2) "The bulk of the examples that follow were taken from computer manuals." In (1) the verb *is* agrees in number with *generation*, the subject of the noun phrase, but in (2) the verb *were* agrees not with the subject *bulk* but with *examples,* a modifier in the noun phrase. In cases like that of (2), which are quite common and which are thoroughly respectable grammatically, we say that the verb has assumed the number that it has by attraction; that is, it has been "attracted" to the noun closest to it in the phrase.

augury/omen: both words refer to a circumstance that functions as a sign or token of future events. The semantic difference between them lies in the fact that there is associated with *omen* a negative connotation, a connotation absent from the semantic coloration of *augury*. Therefore, one usually invokes good auguries and bad omens. Expressions like "This augurs well (is a good augury) for the future" are more likely than "This augurs ill (is a bad augury) for the future." Correspondingly, "This is an evil (or ill) omen for the future" is more likely than "This is a good (or positive) omen for the future." In general, an augury bodes well for the future, an omen bodes ill.

avert/avoid: recently, a person speaking of the aftermath of a hurricane, said, (1) "Most of the damage could have been averted if adequate precautions had been taken." Another person, speaking of the riots that occurred in a European city, said, (2) "The violence could have been averted if adequate police protection had been provided." The use of *averted* seems to be correct in sentence (2) but not entirely so in (1). Why is this? Etymologically, *avert* means "to turn away," but it means this in a transitive sense; that is, it means "to turn (something) away." Not only that: The object, force, or condition that is turned away must be something that is extrinsic to the person or agency that does the averting. Thus, for example, blows can be averted, but not pain; a snub can be averted, but not a humiliation—similarly, violence, but not damage. Against this background, a sentence like (3) "A disaster was averted," in which the word *disaster* allows for interpretation either as the workings of an extrinsic force or as the effect produced on the local habitation, would have to be taken in the former sense. Although the contrast is not rendered absolutely, sentence (3) with *avoid* replacing *avert* would more closely reflect the latter interpretation. In the same way, the intent of sentence (1) would be more properly expressed with *avoid* replacing *avert*.

awhile: in this form, the word is an adverb and so must occur as modifier to a verb: "He stayed awhile," "He read awhile," and so on. The form *while*, in contrast, is a noun meaning "period of time," and as such may be preceded by an article as well as a preposition to form common phrases like "for a while, in a while, after a while," and so forth. One can therefore say either "He slept awhile" or "He slept for a while." To be avoided are expressions like "after awhile" and "He slept for awhile."

back-formation: a derivational process whereby a new word is formed by the deletion of an element at the end of a previously existing word. The process takes two basic forms. In one form (relatively infrequent) the structure of a word is misanalyzed and a new word is formed—by back-formation; in the other and more frequent type, the result of the deletion is the emergence of a new part of speech based on the original form. As an example of the first of these two processes, we may instance the words *pea* and *cherry*. Lying chronologically behind these words are the forms *pease* and Old French *cherise*. These forms were interpreted as plurals, and new singulars, namely *pea* and *cherry*, were derived by back-formation. It is as though words like *ease, exercise,* and *rose* were to be taken as plurals and the new singular forms *ea, exerci,* and *ro* were introduced as singulars (cf. *kudos*).

The other form of back-formation is less idiosyncratic in nature and more productive. A case in point involves the relation between the noun *enthusiasm* and the verb *enthuse*. Historically, the noun was borrowed from the Greek language (and transliterated); only subsequently did the verb appear—formed by back-formation. Without checking the historical background, there is no way to determine whether the relation between a pair of this type is that of normal suffixation or that of back-formation. To make this clear, consider the forms: *write/writer* and *typewrite/typewriter*. From the synchronic (that is, present-day) standpoint, one cannot be sure whether the verb forms came first and the nouns were derived by suffixation or whether the noun forms came into the language first and the verbs were formed by back-formation. The fact is that *write* preceded *writer* but *typewriter* preceded *typewrite*; whereas *writer* is derived (by suffixation) from *write*, *typewrite* is formed from *typewriter* by back-formation. A recently noted back-formation is *surveil*, to subject to surveillance.

baleful/baneful: something is baleful that intends or portends harm or injury; something is baneful that produces harm or injury. Thus, a glance or facial expression may be baleful, an herb or poison baneful. If looks in fact could kill, they might be referred to as baneful. Although baneful things are primarily material, it is possible to speak also of certain nonmaterial things as baneful; compare "The negative criticism that his novel received had a baneful effect on Dillon's subsequent productivity" (although the word *injurious* would probably be preferable in this context).

ban/bar: both verbs mean "to forbid or prohibit entry or access to." They differ, however, in that the prohibition effected by *ban* is typically consequent upon a formal proclamation, law, or edict, whereas that effected by *bar* is usually the result of a physical barrier. A man might be said to be barred from entering the premises of a club or association, whereas he might be banned (from membership) on the basis of regulations pertaining to religious, ethnic, or racial characteristics. Someone who is not a registered Democrat might be barred (i.e., physically prevented) from casting a vote in a Democratic primary, whereas a convicted felon would be banned from voting in any election. On the basis of these considerations, both "They banned his entrance to the premises" and "They barred him from membership in the club" should be regarded as semantically suspect.

beauteous/beautiful: as to the respective meanings of these two words, there is very little that one can adduce to distinguish between them. We can say that *beauteous* has literary overtones, that it would seem out of place for someone in casual conversation to say "I met a beauteous girl at a party last night"; also, that even in literature it is not likely that *beauteous* would be found in predicate adjective position, in sentences, say, like "Regina was a beauteous girl." Rather, it will occur in uses like "Just then the beauteous Regina entered the room," that is, as an epithet. This is a case then in which the usage distinctions derive not so much from nuances of meaning as from considerations of "register," in other words, from the mode, spoken or written, informal or literary, in which the discourse is being conducted.

because of/due to: normally, *because* functions as a conjunction introducing a subordinate clause, to wit: "The Mayor was surprised, because he had not expected such a strong resistance to his proposal." In construction with *of*, however, *because* makes up a compound preposition that, as such, governs a noun phrase: thus, (1) "The store was closed because of the holiday." The phrase *due to* has a similar constitution—that of a compound preposition—the difference lying only in the fact that its first element is an adjective, not a conjunction. Which of these two prepositional compounds would be more appropriate in a given use is determined by quite subtle considerations. Consider (2) "The store was closed due to the holiday." For some reason, sentence (2) does not appear to express the intended sense quite as "happily" as does sentence (1); it seems to imply that the closing was attributable to—in the sense of being caused by— the holiday. In the same way, a sentence like (3) "The store was closed due to a death in the family" would imply that the closing was "caused by" the death. But in a sentence like (4) "The change in the weather was due to the arrival of a cold front from Canada," the phrase *due to* is appropriate, in that the suggestion of causation is here properly motivated. The semantic shading in these sentences seems to reflect the nature and function of the noun phrase that follows the (compound) preposition; it appears that when that phrase describes a condition or an event, *in view* of which the activity of the main clause is seen as taking place, as in (3), then *because of* is preferable, whereas when it describes an action or development *in consequence* of which the activity of the main clause is seen as taking place, then *due to* is preferable, as in (4). Another way to put this is to say that the noun phrase introduced by *because of* indicates a reason for what is described in the main clause, whereas the one introduced by *due to* provides a cause.

Compare now (5) "The store was closed because of the strike" and (6) "The store was closed due to the strike," and consider the grammatical status of the form *closed* in these sentences. One could claim that its status is actually ambiguous: It may be taken either as an adjective modifying *store* or as a past participle, with the agent noun (denoting the person or agency doing the closing) having been omitted. However, it seems to me that taking *closed* as an adjective consists with regarding the prepositional phrase as constituting a reason for the store's being closed and is thus the preferred reading for (5), whereas taking *closed* as a past participle consists with regarding the prepositional phrase as specifying a cause for the store's having been closed and is thus preferred for (6). It would be consistent with the former of these two readings to follow *store* with a slight pause in speech (and perhaps even a comma in writing). By way of casting some additional light on the ambiguous nature of *closed*, consider the sentences "The door was open" and "The door was opened (by Larry)," in which *open* and *opened* correlate with the two senses of *closed* just described.

because **preceded by a comma:** in a sentence in which *because* connects two clauses in the first of which the verb is negated, a lot turns on whether the *because* is or is not preceded by a comma. Consider the sentence "I didn't feel pressure because I was prepared." As it stands, this sentence invites the interpretation "I did feel pressure but it wasn't because I was prepared"; it was perhaps for some other reason—say, because I had a cold or because I had slept badly. What is probably the intended sense of such a sentence is read off it when it is rendered "I didn't feel pressure, because I was prepared." The principle involved here is one of what we might call "scope." Does the scope (the syntactic impulsion) of the phrase "didn't feel pressure" extend through the second clause, or not? Without the comma, it does and therefore allows for the (probably unintended) reading that it was not because I was prepared that I felt pressure; it was (by implication) for some other reason. With the comma, the scope of the phrase is arrested at the comma, and the second clause functions, as it were, nonrestrictively, providing a reason for why I didn't feel pressure. The principle of scope invoked here is the same as that which operates in the case of restrictive and nonrestrictive clause modifiers. Compare (1) "I finally found the book which had fallen behind the desk" with (2) "I finally found the book, which had fallen behind the desk." In (1), the scope of "found the book" extends through the relative clause and has the effect of combining that clause with the preceding phrase, making the object of *found* not simply "the book," but "the book which had fallen behind the desk." In (2), the scope of "found the book" ends at the comma, and the relative clause functions nonrestrictively; its effect in this function is to make an additional, an ampliative, comment about the book.

Following are a few recently noticed instances where the critical role played by the comma is unappreciated and where, as a consequence, the sense of the utterance is grossly deformed. Sentence (1) was a heading that appeared in a well-known magazine: "Every year, some kid makes a movie on a shoestring that gets picked up by Hollywood." Does the author of this sentence really believe that Hollywood picks up a shoestring? Sentence (2) appeared in an important statement of American policy regarding conditions in the Middle East: "We must respond to those who have declared war on peace by waging war on terror." Is it really the case that those who have declared war on peace have done so by waging war on terror? And sentence (3) was in an article about the problems experienced by the children of artists: "Some of the children, now artists themselves, have worked hard to reconcile those roles [i.e., the shift from parent's apprentice to status as peer], choosing to lead creative lives with no certainty that they would succeed." Is such, indeed, the sort of choice—one assured of failure—that they would make? A comma is, to be sure, a simple, rather mundane mark of punctuation, but it can effect by its use syntactic—and hence conceptual—modifications of extreme power and significance. In language, everything counts.

Returning now to the relation between negatives and *because,* let us consider how the absence of a comma in the following sentences produces the need for syntactic recycling: "Don't tax small businessmen because they create jobs"; "I don't think the military will ever respond to him because he's a draft dodger." Both these sentences require the comma. Following is how a statement made by President Clinton in 1996 is cited in a recent issue of the *Wall Street Journal*: "Inflation protection bonds can be a solid rock upon which families build their futures and their dreams. Not a penny of value will ever be lost to anyone who buys them because of inflation" (July 17, 1997). As the passage stands—without the comma before *because,* it conveys the sense that no value (notice the negative) will ever be lost to anyone who buys one of the bonds induced to do so because inflation has set in. The meaning no doubt intended is that no one who buys one of the bonds will suffer lost value as a consequence of inflation later setting in.

(to) **beg the question:** begging the question is, technically, a logical fallacy (Lat. *petitio principii*); it consists in stating as a conclusion what is explicitly or implicitly the question at issue; a variant takes the form of not actually stating the question at issue but of representing it as a thought in a hypothetical clause. In a discussion over whether closing the local library on Tuesdays or Wednesdays would deprive more patrons of service, a woman says, "I think it would be better for the public if the library were closed on Tuesdays." On being asked why she thinks so, she replies, "Well, because then fewer people would suffer." Since the question being addressed is precisely whether fewer people would suffer by the library's being closed either on Tuesdays or on Wednesdays, for someone to say that fewer people would suffer if it were closed on Tuesdays does not answer the question, it begs it; that is, it presents as though it were the conclusion to an argument the very question that was at issue. In a case in which police brutality was being charged, a representative for the defendant, in discussing the circumstances, declared, "The question before us is whether the use of excessive force was justified." Since the purpose of the legal proceedings was precisely to determine whether the police had in fact used excessive force—since that was the very question at issue—the representative's formulation presented as a conclusion what was in fact the question. The inconsistency in this fallacy would perhaps become clearer if rather than referring to it as begging the question, we referred to it instead as the fallacy of asserting the question.

   Illustrating the second form of the fallacy would be a situation in which in a discussion of whether steroids might lead to serious complications, an athlete replies, "If an athlete can take drugs without causing harm to himself, then I don't see why he shouldn't be permitted to take them." Here, in the hypothetical clause that introduces the sentence, there is already taken for granted—begged or argued—the very question that is up for consideration. Another example of this type: In a commercial for a low-commission brokerage firm, a prospective client asks, "What do I have to give up to take advantage of these economies?" The answer: "If you make your own decisions, you give up nothing." Here again, one of the questions at issue would be precisely whether among the services provided by the brokerage firm there would be included the cooperation of a broker with the client in a variety of decisionmaking procedures: stock recommendations, when to buy, when to sell, and so on. All these questions are implicitly (one might also say, illicitly) answered—that is, they are begged—in the *if*-clause that begins the answer to the question.

The reason that this technical problem becomes a question of usage is that there is a widespread tendency to misuse the expression. Fairly commonly, one encounters a use of the expression in a context like the following: A discussion is developed in which a certain number of facts are adduced or conclusions arrived at, after which the arguer will say something like "But this begs the question of why, if the preceding is true, the author did not mention the role that the father played in these developments." A use recently encountered: "As David Burke, the first of Granada's two Watsons, very reasonably remarked, 'If you made Watson too stupid, it begs the question, why should a man of Holmes' intellect put up with him?'" In such cases, to say "This begs the question" is simply a rather pretentious way of saying "This raises (or prompts) the question." At the same time, however, this usage seems to be gaining ground and is apparently here to stay. We might therefore rationalize (and implicitly condone) the usage by calling it a case of folk meaning or folk semantics (cf. folk etymology).

behavior/conduct: both words refer to modes of acting, ways of comporting oneself. There seems to be a difference in their respective references, however. Some indication of the difference may be gleaned by comparing sentences involving the corresponding verb forms. Thus, if we ask "How did Earl Jenkins behave?" we are asking for a description (of his behavior), and the reply might be "He behaved erratically"; whereas if we ask "How did Earl Jenkins conduct himself?" we are asking for a judgment (about his conduct), and the reply might be "He conducted himself well." Continuing along this line, let us now consider the (respective) ways in which our two nouns may be modified. Following is a class of descriptions that may be predicated of behavior: (1) "erratic," "exuberant," "frenetic," "contemptuous"; now a class of descriptions predicable of conduct: (2) "offensive," "irreproachable," "displeasing," "contemptible." On the assumption that these predicates would only with some semantic strain tolerate cross-selection, we might ask what meaning component is common to each set of predicates and try, using this component, to characterize the difference in meaning between our two words. It turns out that common to the predicates in set (1) is the same meaning component that we saw in the case of the verbs: The adjectives in set (1) all have a meaning that describes the action engaged in by an individual, and the adjectives in set (2) all have a meaning that provides a judgment on that action. The distinction drawn here seems to have some semantic warrant, even though it does not appear to be strictly observed in current usage. Is there, in fact, anything semantically disreputable about sentences like (3) "Earl Jenkins' behavior was offensive" or (4) "Earl Jenkins' conduct was erratic"? The answer, it seems, is that although a question might be raised about (4), (3) would occasion no reaction. Thus, this article seems to be concerned with a rather exiguous distinction.

bellicose/belligerent: both words include the semantic component "prone to fighting"; the difference is that *bellicose* orients this meaning toward an individual, *belligerent* toward an organized body, a national or political entity. A person is therefore bellicose, a nation is belligerent. Instead of saying of a person that he is bellicose, we could say that he is pugnacious; instead of saying of a country that it is belligerent, we could say that it is warlike.

bemoan/lament: both words have the meaning "to express pity or grief over something or other." In many contexts our two words function more or less synonymously. Thus, either *bemoaned* or *lamented* could be used in a context like the following: "Audrey . . . her horse's accidental death." Consider now the context (2) "Audrey . . . the accident that led to her horse's death." In (2) it seems that *bemoan* makes a better semantic fit than does *lament*. It appears that *bemoan* is motivated when the pity or grief is over an event that is joined to a consequence, whereas *lament* is motivated when the grief is over the event itself. Syntactically, this means that following *bemoan* there will be a noun phrase followed by a relative clause, whereas following *lament* there will be simply the noun phrase. In the following sentence either of our two words may be used: (3) "Harry spent the evening bemoaning/lamenting his recent divorce," but in the following sentence *lament* would be contraindicated: (4) "Harry spent the evening bemoaning the events that led to his recent divorce."

benign/benignant: *benign* means "of a kindly disposition," *benignant* means "disposed to acting kindly, to performing acts of kindness." The difference between the two meanings is that *benign* refers to a trait or characteristic, *benignant* to a tendency or disposition. One might expect more in the way of actual acts of kindness from a person who was benignant than from one who was simply benign. A benign person might be surmised as being such simply from appearance or manner; a benignant person would be determined as such by actions. Although it is possible to speak of benign neglect, it is not clear that we could speak of benignant neglect.

There is a rather good correlation between these two words and the pair *benevolent* and *beneficent*; thus, a benign person certainly wishes others well, whereas a benignant person is more likely to do others well. As antonyms—disposed in the same four-way set of relations—we have *malign, malignant, malevolent,* and *maleficent.*

beside/besides: *beside* is a preposition meaning "next to, alongside"; *besides* is a conjunction meaning "in addition, moreover, at the same time." Representative uses: "John is standing beside Mary," "John had already had lunch; besides, he heartily disliked shellfish." There is also the idiomatic expression "John was beside himself (with anger, frustration, or some such)," meaning that he was upset, agitated. To be avoided, as solecistic, is the formulation "John was besides himself."

bespeak/betoken: both words mean "to indicate, provide evidence for," but there is a sense of greater concreteness in the meaning of *betoken,* a sense that probably derives from the presence of *token* in its composition. A form of behavior might bespeak kindliness or arrogance, whereas a footprint in the snow would betoken a predator. A more significant difference in the respective meanings appears to be that *bespeak* indicates something that is present at the moment of speaking, whereas *betoken* indicates something that is to materialize. One would say that lightning bespeaks an electrical discharge but that it betokens thunder. Compare also "His conduct bespoke a wealthy background" and "His conduct betokened an imminent loss of control."

biannual/biennial: the former means "twice a year," the latter "every two years." The difference in the vowel (*a/e*) shown by these two forms is traceable to the Latin, which had a form *biennium* for the meaning "a period of two years" and a form *annualis,* the source of our *annual,* to which, the form *biennial* having already been borrowed into English to characterize a period of two years, the prefix *bi-* was added to produce a form meaning "twice in one year." Compare *centennial* and *millennial*, words that, like *biennial*, signal occurrence once in a period of years, the periods for these two words being one hundred and one thousand, respectively.

blend (portmanteau): the name given to a word that is the result of combining or blending elements from two (or more) words: Some examples are *smog* ("smoke" and "fog"); *motel* ("motor" and "hotel"); *chortle* ("chuckle" and "snort"). Lewis Carroll, who coined a number of such words, referred to them as portmanteau words, the motivation for so characterizing them deriving from the fact that a portmanteau (in British usage) is a bag or suitcase that folds open, thus one that is made up of two parts.

bound/boundary: both words refer to a limit of some kind; where, however, the limit defined by *boundary* is essentially physical—a line or a mark of some kind—the limit defined by *bound* may be abstract or implicit, defined not by a line or a mark but, rather, by something like a legal ruling or a social convention. In a sentence recently encountered, namely, "The judge charged that the magistrate had gone beyond the boundaries of his license," we may observe the sort of mistake that results from failure to observe the distinction.

cacoloquy: a neologism, meaning "bad speech," introduced as a term serving to cover the variety of sins and misdemeanors currently being committed against proper usage. At the basis of the coinage are the Greek *kakos*, meaning "bad, evil, ugly" and the Latin *loqui* "to speak." Granted, it is a hybrid formation; but English has many such—largely to its benefit. Motivating its formation are, on the one hand, such words as *cacophony, cacography, cacodyl* and, on the other, words like *colloquy, soliloquy, ventriloquy*. Once the warrant for *cacoloquy* is granted, we can exploit its presence in the lexicon to form such derivatives as *cacoloquial, cacoloquist,* and even—to describe the verbal exchange between two cacoloquists—*cacoloquium*.

calamity/catastrophe: both words are associated with disastrous events, but their use may be distinguished on the basis that the meaning of *catastrophe* is oriented toward an event viewed in its physical dimension, that of *calamity* toward that event viewed in its human dimension. Thus, when we wish our statement to focus on the property damage or destruction caused by the occurrence, we would use *catastrophe*, whereas when we wish our remarks to focus on the personal misfortune or hardship caused by it, we would use *calamity*. The same event, therefore—an earthquake or a hurricane—may be called either a catastrophe or a calamity, the choice of word depending on the viewpoint taken.

canyon/gorge: geologists distinguish between these two types of depression in the earth's surface using the dimensions of breadth and depth: A canyon is wider than it is deep, a gorge is deeper than it is wide. It is on the basis of these comparative dimensions that the Grand Canyon and the Great Gorge (of Alaska) are respectively named.

career/careen: although expressions such as the following are common: "Wildly out of control, the car careened across the median strip" and "Three drunkards emerged from the saloon and careened down the street," some usage experts would question the use of *careen* in these sentences and would recommend that the word *career* be used in its stead. The basic meaning of *careen* is defined in relation to ships and nautical usage in general. Thus, when a ship is made to lean on its side by the force of the wind, it is said to careen; when it is caused to lean on its side for purposes of cleaning or caulking, the ship is said to have been careened. One of the meanings of *career* is "to rush headlong," and it is this meaning that was probably being unconsciously entertained by speakers when they first began to use *careen* in sentences like those just noted (the process no doubt being facilitated by the phonetic similarity that subsisted between the two words).

capacity/capability: *capacity* refers to a general ability to comprehend an issue or perform a task; *capability* implies a reference to one of a set of such abilities. Compare (1) "She has the capacity to run a major corporation" and (2) "Among her capabilities, I would single out as most impressive that of running a major corporation." Sentence (1) focuses on the subject's general competence, sentence (2) highlights one of her specific attributes. To introduce a more subtle but still seemingly significant distinction, one might say that included in the capacity of a body (person, institution, organization) are its abilities, whereas included in the capability of a body are its powers. It would seem to be a semantic shading of this sort that lies behind the recent but growing usage by Defense Department and military establishment personnel in which *capability* has just about displaced *capacity* in various contexts in which we might normally expect the latter term to be used. Thus, consider the following sentences, typical of recent expressions: (3) "Development of our military capability and our economic growth must go hand in hand," (4) "We need the capability to mount sudden and massive attacks against any enemy," and (5) "The navy must have the capability to defend both coastlines simultaneously." What is added to the meanings of these sentences by using *capability* rather than *capacity*? The answer is not obvious, but it seems to me that the element of power (even the word itself) is suggested in all these (and similar) sentences by the use of *capability* rather than *capacity* and that unconsciously or intentionally this suggested element is the consideration that motivates the innovation in usage. Implied by the preferred usage is that reference is being made to things that the military *could* do rather than to things it is merely able to do.

catachresis: a degenerate form of metaphor. In the standard case, a word used metaphorically replaces a word that is normally—that is, literally—used in a particular context to signal a certain meaning. By this criterion, *dishwater*, say, in the sentence "People should try to avoid using dishwater language," is a metaphor in that it is being used instead of a word that would normally occur in this context, say, the word "overused," or "commonplace." In the standard cases of catachresis, however, such as "foot of the mountain," "leg of the piano," and "mouth of the river," it is not clear that the language ever included words specifically referring to those parts of a mountain, piano, or river. Catachreses step in to make good these lexical gaps; they are metaphors by default, we might say.

censor/censure: to censor is to disallow portions or the entireties of books, plays, and the like on the grounds that the disallowed entities transgress moral, political, or religious standards of propriety; to censure is to criticize vehemently or harshly. As a rule, only officially constituted persons or bodies are empowered to act as censors. Therefore, whereas anyone might censure a book, only the censor (or censors) could have censored it, and if we assume that the entire book had been censored, then no one would be in a position to censure it.

ceremonially/ceremoniously: an act performed ceremonially is one performed according to a ceremony, that is, following certain formal or ritual practices, whereas an act performed ceremoniously is one performed with ceremony, meaning with a certain formality of manner. *Ceremonially* relates to the performance of a procedure; *ceremoniously* relates to the performer of the procedure. It would be appropriate to say that John poured out the champagne ceremoniously, meaning that he made an elaborate exercise out of it, but inappropriate to say that he did so ceremonially; the latter formulation would suggest that there was a prescribed or ritual manner of pouring champagne and that John had poured in that manner. It would be appropriate to say that the rites initiating John into a fraternity were carried out ceremonially, that is, following the formal regulations governing this procedure, but it might be inappropriate to say that those rites were performed ceremoniously. The latter formulation would leave the suggestion that those conducting the initiation called attention to the *manner* in which they conducted the initiation, when what was probably intended was that they carried it out according to the procedure prescribed for such exercises.

It might be worth pointing out that the distinction described here is one that derives from a difference in the suffixes *-al* and *-ous*. (This is but one instance of many where suffixes play crucial roles in the distinguishing of meaning.)

certitude/certainty: certitude is a measure of a person's positive feeling about something; certainty is a measure of the degree to which a process or development may be realized. In both cases the degree is that of totality. If someone is certain that something is the case or is to become the case, that person will speak with certitude regarding that case and regard its realization as a certainty. Certitude amounts to complete conviction concerning an actual or theoretical state of affairs, certainty to assessing its status or outcome as an assured fact. Compare "The president, speaking with strong feeling, said it was a certainty that the Republican Party would gain control of the Congress in the next election. But pronouncements made with comparable certitude have been made before and not been realized; certitude does not entail certainty." In the following sentence, uttered by a political figure, the word is misused: "I know this thing is not a certitude, given the position of the chairman."

childish/childlike: oddly enough, neither of these words has much application in the characterizing of a child. Thus, it would be redundant to describe a four-year-old, for example, as childlike. (We wouldn't say a boat was boatlike or a horse, horselike.) Similarly, it would be largely gratuitous to call such a child "childish." (Worthy of remark would be a child's behavior that was "adultish.") These words are used, rather, with adults. In being so used, however, they have decidedly different meanings. We say that a person is childlike or is being childish. In other words, *childlike* refers to a person's temperament, whereas *childish* refers to a person's behavior. And it seems to be looked upon positively for an adult to have a disposition or temperament like that of a child, but negatively for an adult to behave or carry on like a child. To say, for example, of one's sixty-year-old aunt that she is childlike is to suggest a quality of innocence or guilelessness in her temperament, whereas to describe her as childish implies a capricious and unbecoming quality in her behavior.

classic/classical: both words have a variety of senses, but for our purposes we will focus on just two: for *classic*, assume the meaning "of the highest class" and for *classical* "pertaining to, or characteristic of Greek or Roman antiquity" (these meanings being given in most dictionaries). Compare now the following sentences: (1) "The new addition to the Holmes building is a classic of design" and (2) "The new addition to the Holmes building is of classical design." In these sentences the words are properly used. To be avoided, however, are sentences like (3) "This is a classical case of poor management."

cleave/cling: both words mean "to stick to, to adhere," but in their application they differ in significant ways: *Cling* includes among its semantic components the sense not simply of sticking to (something) but of sticking *together*, so that besides saying of a child that it clings to its mother, one can also say that a mother and a child cling to *one another*; in other words, *cling* will be used when the adherence is reciprocal. In this function, *cleave* would not be so happily employed.

When one thing cleaves to another, the sense conveyed is merely one of attachment, whereas when they are said to cling to one another, the sense is one of adhesion, a tighter, more interactive relation. One can say, "Through every adversity, mother and son clung to one another." If *clove* (or *cleaved*) were used in this sentence, the sense would indeed be that they adhered to each other, but the cleaving would be felt as constituted of two separate, independent acts, one by the son and one by the mother, whereas with *cling* the sense is that of a joint, reciprocal, almost embrace interactivity. Consistent with this analysis is the fact that in the following two expressions, the pairing seems appropriate: "Arthur clove to his principles," "Arthur clung to his prejudices"; the sense of appropriateness derives, I would suggest, from the fact that principles enjoy an independent existence, whereas prejudices are personal and thus more closely integrated with the individual.

The difference in the suggested force of the adherence finds a correlation in the way in which the reciprocity might be indicated grammatically: Thus, one would tend to say "Mother and son clove to each other" but "Mother and son clung to one another," where *each* and *one* in the respective phrases correlate nicely with the separateness and solidarity implied, respectively, by *cleave* and *cling*. (As a rule, one is supposed to use *each other* when the distribution is between two people, and *one another* when it involves more than two, so that, strictly speaking, the distinction drawn here is not a sanctioned one; intuitively, however, I think that there is justification for it.)

climatic/climactic: the former of these two terms is derived from *climate*, the latter from *climax*, so that one can speak of poor climatic conditions or of a certain climactic development. Compare "The climatic conditions that summer were not favorable for the growing of grapes" and "The climactic developments of that summer focused the world's attention on the problems caused by the unrestricted use of pesticides."

comparable to/analogous to: a topped ball to third base that a batter beats out is comparable to a bloop fly over the first baseman's head: Both are types of scratch hit. In other words, they are two species of the same genus. We therefore say "a topped ball that goes for a single is comparable to a bloop fly over the infield." But if we compare a pitcher's winning twenty games in a season with a batter's hitting forty home runs, different types of excellence are involved—for a pitcher and a hitter, respectively. Thus, these feats represent species of different genera. It would, therefore, be correct to say "A twenty-game season for a pitcher is analogous to a forty-home-run season for a hitter." The point is that when the comparison is of such a nature that it comprises three terms (two species and a genus), then *comparable* is the word to use; when it comprises four terms (two species and two genera), the relation requires the word *analogous*. Compare "Tendinitis for a pianist is analogous to elbow strain for a golfer."

comparatively/relatively: compare the following sentences: (1) "The store was comparatively quiet" and (2) "The store was relatively quiet." (1) would be used when the store was quiet in comparison to other stores, (2) when the store was quiet relative to itself, that is, in relation to a standard derived from conditions that generally obtained in the store. Now compare (3) "The store was comparatively spacious" and (4) "The store was relatively spacious." According to the criterion adduced in connection with sentences (1) and (2), sentence (4) should be felt as semantically grating, in that the store's size is a constant factor, and therefore the question of conditions that generally obtain is pointless. However, a sentence like (5) "The store had been made . . . more spacious" should, according to the distinction drawn here, accept either of the two words: with *comparatively* the meaning would be that the store had been made more spacious in comparison with the space in other stores; with *relatively* the meaning would be that it had been made more spacious relative to the space that it previously occupied.

competence/efficiency: strictly speaking, competence is a measure of the ability to perform a task; efficiency is a measure of the success achieved in the performance of a task. When we say someone is competent, we mean that the person has a certain capacity, is *capable* of doing certain things. We say that such a person is efficient after observing that person doing those things and doing them well. In consistency with this analysis, we would say that a person who lacks the requisite ability to perform a certain task is incompetent, but that a person who performs the task but does it poorly is inefficient. Furthermore, it would follow that an incompetent person cannot be efficient at a task but can be inefficient even though competent. If this analysis is correct—if competence refers to an ability, not a practice—then there should be something suspect about the adverbial form of *competent*; it should not be appropriate, that is, to say something like "Helen performed the task competently." But of course this, plus many other examples running counter to the distinction drawn here, represents perfectly acceptable usage. Therefore, the foregoing analysis, despite the support it receives from (a perhaps overpunctilious) semantic intuition, should probably be more borne in mind than applied in practice. However, there is something fundamentally correct about the distinction drawn here. Why, for example, does (1) "Fielder's work was competent" make a weaker claim about Fielder's qualifications than does (2) "Fielder's work was efficient"? Thus, we could add "merely" in (1) but not in (2).

competition/competitiveness: compare (1) "There existed between Freddy Harrison and Beansie Seltzer a strong sense of competition" and (2) "There was manifested between Freddy Harrison and Beansie Seltzer a strong element of competitiveness." Why is it that the exchange of the words *competition* and *competitiveness* in these two sentences would seem to disturb the semantic equilibrium that informs them as they stand? Or, to put it another way, why is it that *existed* is semantically compatible with *competition* and that *competitiveness* motivates a change to *was manifested*? The correlation apparently follows from the fact that *competition* refers to an abstract quality, of which existence can be predicated but whose reality cannot be demonstrated, whereas *competitiveness* implies a practical activity, whose manifestation can be observed.

complacent/complaisant: *complacent* means "pleased or satisfied with how things are, with how they affect one's self"; *complaisant* means "attempting to please or satisfy." *Complacent* thus refers to a state (placidity) of mind, *complaisant* to a disposition to behave or conduct oneself in a certain way, namely, to act in a manner that pleases or satisfies others. Compare "Dorothy is a complacent person" and "Dorothy has a complaisant personality." With *complacent* is associated the component "pleased," with *complaisant* the component "pleasing"; we are to understand "pleased" in this connection, however, in its adjectival function, that is, as describing Dorothy's state of mind, not her reaction to what has happened to her; in contrast, we are to understand "pleasing" in this connection in its participial (not its adjectival) function, that is, as describing the efforts made by Dorothy, not the effect that those efforts may have had upon others.

complement/supplement: both words signify an addition of some kind. The meaning difference turns on whether the addition serves to complete something or form with it a whole, in which case the addition is a complement, or whether the addition is to something that may already be regarded as complete or as constituting a whole, when the addition is a supplement. Males complement females in the class of human beings, children supplement parents in the formation of a family. Consider the case of wine being added to a dinner. Compare (1) "Wine was served as a complement to the dinner" with (2) "Wine was served as a supplement to the dinner." As variants we have (3) "Wine was served to complement the dinner" and (4) "Wine was served to supplement the dinner." The inference from (1) and (3) is that the dinner was satisfactory when considered on its own, that is, as a whole or individual unit, and that it was complemented (made a larger whole) by the addition of the wine. From (2), and more definitely from (4), however, the inference may be drawn that the dinner taken by itself was incomplete, unsatisfactory, and that it was only brought to wholeness by the addition of the wine. From (1) and (3) we conclude simply that the dinner was complemented, from (2) and (4), however, we infer that it needed to be supplemented.

complex/complicated: common to both terms is the meaning "involved, intricately designed or constructed," but *complicated* adds to this general meaning the sense of "perverse, intractable, resistant to analysis." Something complex (a structure, design, or argument) may, for all its subtlety or intricacy, be well organized, logically constructed; a thing that is complicated will have, overlaid on its fundamental intricacy, something irregular, perverse, asymmetrical, a factor that makes analysis or solution additionally difficult. In "Peter leads a very complex life," Peter's life, although involved, may for all that still be systematic, well organized—importantly, it may follow a pattern or design established entirely by Peter; however, in "Peter leads a very complicated life," there is the implication that some of the factors complicating Peter's life have their source in people or considerations that act independently of Peter.

complimentary/complementary: this article is occasioned by the following notice published by a large corporation: "We are interested in the aggressive acquisition of complimentary companies." A compliment is an expression of praise or admiration, so that something is complimentary when it has the property embodied in such an expression; a complement, however, is a factor whose addition produces completeness or perfection in something, so that what is complementary has the property of producing such an effect. A remark praising your hat is complimentary; for some tastes, a feather added to the hat is complementary. The firm that printed the notice quoted here might have been interested in acquiring companies that embodied properties praising or admiring it but was much more likely to have been interested in the acquisition of companies whose addition would make of it a more complete and comprehensive commercial enterprise.

comportment/deportment: both words refer to a person's behavior or mode of conduct, but *deportment* has, added to its meaning, the sense of action or activity, a sense that is missing from the meaning of *comportment*. Thus, "Louie Cimino's comportment was dignified"; "Bobby Keehn's deportment was frenetic"; compare also "Jerry Harper comported himself quietly/with dignity"; "Jerry Harper deported himself vigorously/with animation."

compose/comprise/constitute: these three words share as one of their component meanings the sense of making up as a part some whole or entity. Thus, one can say, with little difference in the general sense conveyed, "The orchestra is composed of (or "is comprised of" or "is constituted by") ninety musicians." There are, however, subtle differences in the respective meanings of the three terms, so that in certain contexts one or another of them is more appropriately used; thus, *compose* is to be preferred when the parts of the whole being assembled are regarded as nonconcrete, more general; when the parts are regarded as concrete and specific, then *constitute* is more appropriate; compare (1) "Water is composed of hydrogen and oxygen" and (2) "Water is constituted by molecules of hydrogen and oxygen." In (2) *constituted (by)* conveys the sense that the whole is being built up by the parts, thus that it results from their combination; whereas with *compose* (in 1), the sense is one of the whole simply consisting of its component parts.

From the standpoint of the relation between part and whole, *comprise* has a dual meaning; as just shown, it may be used more or less with the meaning of our other two terms (particularly that of *compose*); it may also be used to indicate not the building up (the forming) of a whole from its parts but instead take its meaning from the standpoint of the whole as comprehending or encompassing the parts. Thus, one can say "Water is comprised of oxygen and hydrogen" or "Water comprises (the elements) oxygen and hydrogen." The latter is probably its original sense (cf. the principal parts of the French *comprendre*).

compulsion/impulsion: compare "Ottie Langnas is a compulsive eater" and "Ottie Langnas is an impulsive eater." A compulsive eater is compelled by an exterior force to eat and, the force being unremitting, eats constantly; an impulsive eater is impelled (has an impulse) to eat and, the impulse occurring sporadically, eats only from time to time. The difference between the two types of psychological dependency is that a compulsion is a reaction to an outer pressure, whereas an impulsion obeys an inner prompting. Compare as reinforcing this difference: A man walking impels himself (to go) forward, a man jostled is compelled (to move) forward; further, people impel themselves to write, a deadline compels them to write (notice the nicely correlating use of reflexive pronouns in the *impel* sentences.

concept/conception: both words refer to ideas or notions, but a concept is a more definite, more unitary, more complete type of notion than is a conception, which is more of an ideational structure with a potential for realization—rather like a schema. A concept is complete in the ideational space that it occupies, but a conception, although its boundaries may be well defined, contains within its bounds phases that remain to be satisfied. A person having the concept of universal brotherhood, say, would, in having that concept, have a clear idea of what such a state of affairs would look like. Another person, who had a conception of universal brotherhood, would have an idea of how that goal is to be achieved and would have formed, as components of the conception, proposals for the elimination of certain barriers, for the institution of various programs, and measures to insure the cooperation of the relevant parties—all these, and other considerations, going to make up the conception. A concept is a blueprint of how something is; a conception is a draft of how something might be.

confirm/corroborate: both words mean "to strengthen, provide support for," but *corroborate* is used in a narrower context, usually by way of providing support for testimony in a legal proceeding. However, testimony of a more general sort, say, that of the details in a story or description, may also be corroborated. *Confirm* is used by way of lending support to a much wider array of things: A prejudice may be confirmed, a hunch, a weather report, even an unfavorable impression. A major difference between the two supporting functions is that corroboration implies an application to verbal statements or written documents, whereas confirmation is not so restricted in its application.

congruent/congruous: both words mean "agreeing or corresponding with," but *congruent* has this meaning in a stricter, more technical sense. Thus, two geometric figures that agree in every respect, one being exactly superimposable upon the other, are congruent; two right angles, for example, are congruent angles. In mathematics, two numbers that, upon division by the same divisor leave the same remainder, are congruent—for example, 7 and 42 are congruent by virtue of the fact that on division by 5 they both leave the remainder 2. When the type or degree of correspondence is looser, more general, *congruous* is used: Thus, the thoughts of an author of a book and its publisher might be congruous—in the sense that both wish for a large sale, say. Or two plans for the stimulation of the economy, although differing in details, might be congruous in the general measures that they propose. The distinction drawn here applies equally to the negative forms of these words; the consequence is that *incongruent* would not likely appear in other than technical speech, whereas expressions like the following, involving *incongruous* are quite common: "The use of Doric columns at the front of the building is incongruous with its otherwise Gothic facade" or "I find it incongruous, given your past history, that you now want to live in the country."

connive/conspire: one connives at something but conspires with somebody. Compare (1) "Stanley connived at Harry's misrepresentation of the facts" and (2) "Stanley conspired with Harry to misrepresent the facts." In (1), Stanley remained silent as Harry proceeded with the misrepresentation, thus, while tacitly condoning it, being able to deny responsibility; in (2), Stanley took an active role in planning the misrepresentation, making himself susceptible, along with Harry, of any blame that might accrue. These different consequences follow on the two acts because connivance is an act of omission, conspiracy one of commission. The words, it might be added, need not necessarily be used in contexts such that their connotations are negative; one can connive at producing a positive or favorable outcome, just as one can conspire to bring such an outcome about.

connotation/denotation: if we ask whether words refer to things or represent the ideas that we have about things, the answer would seem to be that they perform both these functions. Any account of meaning, therefore, must enable us to deal with these two aspects of a word's signifying capacity. In his *System of Logic,* John Stuart Mill used the words *denotation* and *connotation* to comprehend those two aspects of a word's expressive range. By *denotation,* he meant the word's reference to the things it designated; by *connotation,* the general ideas that a speaker has about the designated things, that is, the common attributes of the referent that the word brought to mind. The denotation of the word *horse,* for example, would range over the set of horses—refer to them singly or in total. The connotation would consist of the attributes that occurred to the speaker in using the word; to be sure, the attributes do not add up to a well-defined set, but some features of a horse would figure in the representations of most speakers—say, that a horse has four legs, that it has hoofs, that its diet consists of plants and grains, and so on. Versions of this dual view of a word's meaning occur in many semantic theories of the present day.

The signification of the two terms began to be modified in the twentieth century in consequence of the use to which they were put by literary critics, whose critical needs were not satisfied by a semantic account that allocated two such general dimensions to the meaning of words; they particularly felt an inadequacy when the categories were applied to words as they occurred in poetry. In the course of their critical practice, the applicability of *denotation* was extended so as to comprehend both the earlier denotation and connotation, and *connotation* was employed to register a wide variety of responses, encompassing an array that embraced suggestions, emotions, sensations, associations, and any other evocations that might be stimulated by the words occurring in a poetic text. Under this sort of dispensation, occurrence of the word *horse* in a poem might "connote" to the reader a youthful ride on a horse-drawn sleigh, a winning ticket at the race track, a recollection of fear in the presence of an agitated animal, the memory of a horse grazing in a field, the smell of a stable, and any number of other possible associations. The difference between the two approaches—at least as far as the role played by connotation is concerned—is that in the earlier, Millean sense, there is at least the aim that the connotations of words should enjoy a more or less general acceptance, whereas in the new approach the connotations of words lose generality and become a function of the accidents that have occurred in an individual's experience.

It is the second sense of *connotation* that is employed in most discourse today. People say things like "I don't like the connotations in your last remark." The fact that in sentences like these the connotation is construed as affecting the speaker as an individual shows that *connotation* is understood in the extended, less specific sense that it has developed in the field of literary criticism.

consist of/in: the function of *consist* is to combine or link sentence elements that lie on either side of it; depending on whether it is followed by *of* or *in*, that connection assumes a different value. When followed by *of,* elements that follow *consist* are understood as composing or constituting an element that precedes it; thus, "Water consists of hydrogen and oxygen molecules," "The United States consists of fifty states." When followed by *in,* what follows is understood as a gloss, an equivalent of an element that precedes *consist:* "Anarchy consists in a disrespect for laws," "His personal philosophy consists in an admiration for unconventional values." In the following sentence, both functions are represented: "The United States government consists of three branches: the executive, the legislative, and the judiciary; its superiority over other forms of government consists in the checks and balances that each of these branches exercises over the others." In general, we might say that *consist of* means "is made (up) of, is composed of" and that *consist in* means "resides in, lies in."

consolation/solace: solace is a form of comfort given to one who is in sorrow or distress; consolation is an act of offering such comfort or the result of such comfort having been provided. The presence of this "actional" property in the meaning of *consolation* stems no doubt from its having been derived from the verb *console*. It appears then that the use of one or the other of our two words will depend on whether there is involved in the comfort provided a sense of prior action. Compare (1) "The fact that his rabbi sent him a telegram brought a measure of consolation to Harvey in his grief" and (2) "The telegram that his rabbi sent him was a solace to Harvey in his grief." Perhaps not a great deal of semantic nicety would be sacrificed if our two words were interchanged in sentences (1) and (2) (although some would). But consider a sentence like (3): "When Harvey's business failed, he looked to his friends for consolation." If *solace* were to be used in this sentence instead of *consolation*, the meaning would be changed in a way that would alter the sense that (3) conveys about Harvey's state of mind. As it stands, the sentence suggests that Harvey wanted "shows" of concern, the actual proffering of sympathy; replacing *consolation* with *solace* in sentence (3) would suggest, however, that Harvey's primary need was, rather, to attain the state of mind that would result from such tenders of sympathy.

constrain/restrain: among the meanings given for *constrain* is "to repress or restrain"; among those for *restrain* is "to keep in check, repress." There is therefore a certain overlap between the meanings of these two words. Consider the use of the words in the following sentences: (1) "I was constrained against entering the discussion," (2) "I was restrained from entering the discussion," (3) "I was constrained against entering the discussion by a feeling of intellectual inadequacy," (4) "I was restrained from entering the discussion by a warning expression on Don Goldenberg's face," (5) "Throughout the discussion, I felt myself laboring under a certain constraint," (6) "Throughout the discussion, I was aware of operating under a certain restraint," (7) "Something constrained me against expressing my actual views on the subject," and (8) "Something restrained me from expressing my actual views on the subject." Determining the use of one or the other word in these sentences is whether the check or repression—the "-straint"—comes from within, from a trait of character or some behavioral predisposition, or whether it derives from a condition originating outside ourselves. In the former case, *constraint* is motivated; in the latter case, *restraint*. Compare (5) and (6), where this consideration underlies the use of one and the other of the two words; similarly in (7) and (8), we are led to infer that the repressing "something" is respectively a factor intrinsic to and extrinsic to the speaker. Compare as making this distinction explicit (9) "What constrained me against denouncing him was my sense of fair play" and (10) "What restrained me from denouncing him was my recollection of his earlier generosity." The prepositions respectively used with the two words consist with the distinction being drawn here: Thus, one is inhibited against, but is prevented from, doing something.

contemporary/contemporaneous: the semantic component common to these two forms is "pertaining to the same time," but whereas *contemporary* can be predicated of persons, conditions, or events, *contemporaneous* is predicable only of occurrences or events. This difference in predicability derives from the fact that the specific meaning of *contemporary* is "existing at the same time as," whereas that of *contemporaneous* is "occurring at the same time as." Thus, two persons or conditions can be said to be contemporary with each other, but not contemporaneous with each other; in comparison, two events can be said to be contemporaneous with each other, but not (as happily) contemporary with each other. Compare (1) "Newton's career was contemporary with the founding of the Royal Society" and (2) "Newton's discovery of gravity was contemporaneous with the founding of the Royal Society." In (1), the use of *contemporary* causes us to think that Newton's career is something that existed, not something that occurred, and in (2), the use of *contemporaneous* is consistent with our thinking of Newton's discovery as something that happened—as an event.

It is because of the specific meaning mentioned earlier, that is, the emphasis on occurrence—in other words, on an action of some sort—in its meaning that *contemporaneous* gives rise to an adverbial form. One could therefore rephrase sentence (2) as "Newton's discovery of gravity occurred contemporaneously with the founding of the Royal Society." However, although the dictionary offers *contemporarily* as an adverbial form, it is not clear what function is served by that form, given the semantic orientation of *contemporary* toward mere existence.

contempt/disdain: both words signify a feeling of strong disapproval mingled frequently with scorn or distaste, but contempt is a more engaged, more involved feeling than disdain. Compare (1) "Richard treated his associates with contempt" and (2) "Richard treated his associates with disdain." If Richard has contempt for his associates, as in (1), that feeling will probably make itself manifest in certain acts or remarks of his; Richard's feeling of disapproval so exercises him that he will be unable to confine it to his thoughts. The feeling (disdain) that Richard has for his associates in (2), however, has the consequence that he has as little as possible to do with them; he deems them not worthy of his notice. A person who is beneath contempt is thus not beneath disdain.

continual/continuous: both forms mean "without interruption," but *continuous* is stricter in projecting this sense. Thus, *continual* may be used of a sustained but intermittent (i.e., noncontinuous) state or condition; compare "He was in continual pain" to the sense of unremittingness in "The pain was continuous." The distinction is perhaps more pronounced in the adverbial pair: Compare "After falling off the chair, Johnny cried continuously for three hours," that is, without letup or interruption, and "After the death of his dog Towser, Johnny cried continually for three weeks," that is, off and on. If *continually* were substituted in the former sentence, the result would be a mere modification of the meaning, but if *continuously* were substituted in the latter, a reaction of skepticism would not be unwarranted.

Recently, a commentator said of a well-known movie director, "He was continuously rediscovering the cinema, reinventing it, exploring its unique properties." Discoveries are punctual events; they occur at particular points of time; such being their nature, they cannot take place continuously. To remark the director's consistent originality and freshness of approach, the commentator should have used *continually*. Compare also the following sentence, where the same replacement is indicated: "Each of the entities has its own car mafia, and they're in continuous touch with one another, sometimes even by walkie-talkie."

convene/convoke: consider the following sentences: "The mayor's aides convened in his office" and "The mayor convoked his aides to a meeting in his office." In these two sentences the words are used in accordance with their etymological meanings, *convene* from the Latin *convenire* "to come together" and *convoke* from the Latin *convocare* "to call together." Grammatically, moreover, the words differ in that *convene* is intransitive, whereas *convoke* is transitive. Thus, from the standpoint of both etymological background and transitivity, there is a lack of precision in the common usage reflected in such sentences as "The mayor convened a meeting of his aides" or "The mayor convened a meeting in his office." But this usage is apparently here to stay. In fact, most dictionaries allow a transitive sense for *convene*.

convex/concave: *convex* refers to a surface that curves outward; *concave* to a surface that curves inward. Think of the half of a hollow rubber ball. Its outer surface is convex, its inner surface concave. Or think of the letter C. Approaching from the left, the letter's surface is convex; approaching from the right, its surface is concave. As it happens, the inner surface of a cave is concave. However, this is not just a lucky coincidence, meant to provide us with a handy mnemonic. There is a common etymological element in *cave* and *concave*, deriving from the Latin *cavus*, meaning "hollow."

credence/credibility: something is credible to the extent that it is worthy of belief, so that credibility is worthiness, in general, of belief; credence is an acknowledgment of such worthiness. Although both statements and people may be judged credible, by way of acknowledging this fact one lends credence to a statement and accords credibility to a person. A recent newspaper column ended with the sentence "Those whose ethos is a seamless garment of respect for life, not one of subjugation and control, must speak loudly if their cause is to have any credence." A cause cannot acknowledge or confer believability; it may, however, be worthy of belief. For this reason, the last word in the sentence just quoted should be "credibility."

critical/crucial: compare the phrases "a critical experiment" and "a crucial experiment." As between the two types of experiment, more would be thought to ride on the crucial than on the critical experiment. Whereas in the testing of a hypothesis, say, a critical experiment might have extremely significant implications, performing a crucial experiment would make or break the hypothesis. Compare now: (1) "The summer that Valerie spent in Paris represented a critical stage in her intellectual development" and (2) "The summer that Valerie spent in Paris represented a crucial stage in her intellectual development." From (1) we infer that Valerie's intellectual development was significantly influenced by the summer that she spent in Paris, and she might tell us, for example, that she had then decided to read more philosophy; from (2) we infer that the summer was a watershed experience in her development, and she might tell us that as a direct consequence of that summer she had determined to become a philosopher.

cult/sect: both words refer to a group of people who are united by belief in a common religious, ideological, or philosophical principle. The group constituting a sect usually represents a faction within a larger community of adherents, its defining characteristic being a focus on a particular aspect of, or departure from, the general doctrine. The various denominations of the Protestant Church, for example—Methodist, Lutheran, Baptist, Unitarian, and so forth—are regarded as individual sects of that church. A cult, however, need not be part of a larger group; it is usually, rather, an independent and unaffiliated body. Thus, the group of followers that congregated around the preacher Jim Jones in Guyana in the late 1970s constituted a cult. The same is true of the Branch Davidians, the followers of David Koresh, many of whom perished in the flames in Waco. Likewise, any other present-day group that adhered to the tenets of a doctrine propounded by an individual who claimed divinity would be a cult. An important difference between the two types of organization is that a sect is as a rule defined by some doctrinal difference, a cult by allegiance to a leading idea or commanding personality.

cultured/cultivated: what difference is there in saying of a person that she is cultured or in saying of that person that she is cultivated? What difference in meaning is there between the sentences (1) "Nancy is a cultured woman" and (2) "Nancy is a cultivated woman"? A clue lies in the fact that whereas *cultured* in (1) is an adjective, *cultivated* in (2) has both an adjectival and a participial sense. Thus, we read (1) as meaning that Nancy has absorbed culture, has become, has made herself, is, cultured, but we may read (2) as meaning that Nancy has undergone cultivation, has been made cultivated. The difference is that culture is acquired, by study and application; cultivation is developed, by training and exposure. The distinction cannot be made hard and fast—there is considerable overlap—but we might venture the following as guidelines: reading great literature, studying history, learning to play a musical instrument—engaging in such activities will make a person more cultured. Extensive travel, learning foreign languages, visiting art museums—experiences of this sort will make a person more cultivated. The acquisition of culture, we might say, is a process engaged in by a person; the development of cultivation is a process undergone by a person. We speak of a pearl as cultured, the pearl being largely of its own making, but we speak of an orchid variety as cultivated, the orchid having been tended (cultivated) so as to ensure its particular realization.

cynic/skeptic: in the context of certain circumstances, say, that of a person reporting the contents of a conversation, presenting a plan for a particular project, or providing an account of a given situation, a cynic would withhold assent from the person's testimony; that reservation is based, however, on the cynic's belief that what people say is determined not by what they actually believe to be the case but by their desire to promote selfish ends, with the result that their reports of events are skewed or distorted so as to serve those ends. Cynics, in other words, doubt because they question motives. Skeptics likewise doubt reports of what they hear or read. In their case, however, the doubt arises not necessarily because they question a reporter's motives but rather on the basis that they have a doubting nature; they simply doubt what is presented to them. Given an account of what took place at a certain party, for example, the skeptic will raise questions about the reporter's account, the cynic will have questions about the reporter. These considerations apply, of course, to the meanings of the adjectival derivatives *cynical* and *skeptical*.

damp/dampen: consider a structure like (1) "Nothing that Vinnie might say could _____ Henry's enthusiasm for the projected vacation." Is any semantic difference entailed by the use of one or the other of our two forms in the slotted position? It seems that the intended sense—that of a restraining, checking, or depressing of Henry's enthusiasm—would be conveyed just as well were we to use either *damp* or *dampen*. If we look into the derivational backgrounds of the two forms, we can see a reason for this. Both forms have underlying them the adjective *damp*. The verbal *dampen* is formed by adding to the adjective the suffix *-en*, in the same way as are derived the verbals *quicken, sweeten, moisten,* and so on, from their respective underlying adjectives; the verbal *damp*, in its turn, is derived from the adjective by functional shift, in the same way as are verbals like *to cool, to wet, to warm,* and so forth. We thus have two different verbal forms with the same underlying base. Whatever difference of meaning we might ascertain would have to be a function of the different manners of derivation. In this connection, then, we might point to the fact that the addition of the *-en* suffix to an adjective produces a form whose meaning is something like "to *produce* the condition that the adjective describes," so to quicken is to *make* quick, to moisten is to *make* moist, and so on. From this point of view, *dampen* might be said to indicate its primary meaning—namely, to make damp, that is, slightly moist or wet—by virtue of its being used as a verb and then to project a reinforcement of this meaning through use of the suffix *-en.* Inasmuch, then, as the form *damp* does not incorporate the reinforced meaning "to make moist," we might conclude that for the expression of secondary notions like checking, restraining, or depressing, the kind of meaning indicated for (1), the form *damp* is preferable.

decline/refuse: this article was prompted by an announcement that football referees make when, on a play that gains significant ground for the offensive team, the team on the defense has incurred a penalty, one, however, involving less yardage than the ground gained—say, fifteen yards, when the play has gained twenty-eight. In such cases, the offensive team has an option: It may accept either the penalty or the result of the play. On consultation with the offensive team, the referee will announce its preference. With some referees the announcement takes the form "Penalty is refused," with others it is "Penalty is declined." Is any distinction implied by these different versions? Is there a basis for choosing between them? Dictionaries provide the following definitions: for *decline:* "withhold or deny consent to do, enter into or upon, and so on," also "to refuse to do or accept something"; for *refuse:* "to decline to accept (something offered)," and also "to decline to do, accept, give, or allow." As can be seen, the definitions are largely overlapping. But let us look at the situation. Presumably, the referee asks the offensive team's captain, "Will you take (or do you want) the play or the penalty?" And the captain replies, "We'll take the play." Thus, it is not the case that the penalty has been offered as such, in which case the captain could refuse to accept it. The case is, rather, that the penalty has been offered as an option, and it has been that option that the captain has declined. There is, however, something question-begging about these conclusions, so let us consider the question in a little more detail. Although it may occur followed by a simple object, in its fundamental syntax *refuse,* along with such verbs as *agree, expect, intend,* and the like, takes an infinitive phrase as object, as in "I refuse to accept that offer." This syntactic predilection is the inverse of that displayed by *decline,* which, fundamentally, takes a simple noun phrase as object, as in "I decline that offer." To be sure, both verbs have developed reciprocal uses, so that such expressions as "I refuse your offer" and "I decline to accept your offer" pass syntactic muster. Basically, however, the underlying syntax of the two verbs is such that one declines (or accepts) something that is offered; one refuses (or agrees) to accept something offered. If we return now to the empirical situation, when the question put to the captain is "Will you take the play or the penalty?" he does not refuse to accept the penalty and agree, as it were, to accept the play; rather, he simply declines the penalty and thereby implicitly accepts the play. Conclusion: Referees should say "The penalty has been declined."

definite/definitive: *definite* means "clear, sharply delineated"; *definitive* means "complete, final, ultimate." A definite program would be one that set out clearly the goals of the program and that recommended steps for the carrying out of that program; a definitive program would be one that provided for the project envisaged a complete set of procedures—such that no revisions, additions, or supplements are contemplated for the successful carrying out of that program. A definite program might be one of a number of programs for the same project, all of which display the character of definiteness but no one of which would necessarily be successful; a definitive program, however, would not likely have any congeners and would carry with it a presumption of success.

degenerate/deteriorate: compare the following two sentences: (1) "Our relationship had degenerated from one in which we confided in each other without reservation to one in which we no longer spoke freely about any of our affairs" and (2) "Our relationship had deteriorated to the point where we hardly spoke to each other." It seems to me that the exchange of our two words in these sentences would render each one slightly less precise; to degenerate means "to decline in value, to move lower on a scale," but to deteriorate means "to worsen, to become lowered, or be reduced in value." Both meanings, as we see, involve a downward movement; the meaning of *degenerate*, however, works within the movement phase of the process, whereas that of *deteriorate* falls on its conclusion. Therefore, in sentence (1), where the two states of the relationship are mentioned, the distance between them is implied, and since the meaning of *degenerate* describes a downward traversal of a distance, it is the appropriate word; in sentence (2), the focus is on the concluding stage of a process—on its end point—and here the meaning of *deteriorate*, with its implication of a reduction to a concluding state, makes it the appropriate word to use.

deictics: a class of words whose semantic value is not a matter of meaning but, rather, is determined by the *use* to which they are put. A (nondeictic) word like *horse*, for example, has a meaning, which meaning it has regardless of the nonlinguistic context in which it is used. On the contrary, the meaning of a deictic like *yesterday* can be determined only by considering its context of use. Uttered on July 8th, the word means one thing, on November 12th another, on April 23rd another, and so on. Of course, it is possible to define *yesterday* as meaning "the day before the day on which the word is uttered." But this definition only drives home the point—that in order to arrive at the meaning of deictics, it is necessary to take account of the *non*-linguistic environment in which they are uttered. A corollary of this requirement is that the meaning of deictics varies with their use. Consider a sample sentence: "Yesterday I joined the Golden Bears." The date when I joined the Golden Bears cannot be learned from the sentence itself. In order to know that, it is necessary to know when—the date on which—I uttered the sentence. Notice also that the *I* in the sentence refers to whoever happens to be the author of the sentence. Deictics include, among other classes, temporal and locative adverbs, personal and demonstrative pronouns, tense words, and a few others.

delay/postpone: compare (1) "Construction was delayed by a shortage of electrical wiring" and (2) "Construction was postponed by an order from the foreman." The general difference is that various things may cause a delay, but a postponement will result from the action of a person. Compare (3) "Work on the project was delayed by a blizzard," (4) "Work on the project was postponed by a blizzard," and (5) "Work on the project was postponed because of a blizzard." Sentences (3) and (5) pass muster, but sentence (4) raises the question "What could a blizzard *do* that would result in work being stopped?" From (5) we draw the inference that because of the blizzard, someone decided that the work should be stopped.

demagoguery/demagogy: although the original, primary meaning of *demagogue* is that of a leader of the common people (Greek *agein* "to lead," *demos* "the people"), its developed meaning, and the meaning that it has in most contemporary uses, is that of a person, usually a politician, who enlists people's support or arouses them to action by the use of impassioned, hortatory, or inflammatory rhetoric. The usage consideration involves not the word *demagogue*, however, but rather whether a person who uses the language in order to arouse listeners is indulging in demagoguery or in demagogy. This question is pertinent since we hear and read both "This is demagoguery of the rankest sort" and "This is demagogy of the rankest sort." Another example: "Each of the speakers, instead of discussing the issues, has resorted to a shameful display of demagoguery" and "Each of the speakers, instead of discussing the issues, has resorted to a shameful display of demagogy." Both forms enjoy lexicographical sanction in such uses, but it should be possible to ascertain a basis for distinguishing between them. Thus, *demagoguery* could be used to describe speech that is demagogic, *demagogy* to describe behavior or conduct that is demagogic. Of course, the question arises whether behaving like a demagogue embraces any more than speaking like one, in which case we would be drawing a distinction where there is no difference. But if a man spends all his time hatching plans to arouse the populace, has meetings, organizes followers, sends out mailings, all with the single purpose of maximizing the demagogic effect that his addresses will have upon his audiences, we might say of such a man that he is practicing demagogy. Against this background, different inferences would be warranted from the following two sentences: (1) "Candidate A practices demagoguery in its purest form" and (2) "Candidate A practices demagogy in its purest form." The practical conclusion to be drawn from this discussion is that in the paired sentences provided earlier in this article the preferred form is *demagoguery*.

depend/rely: we may observe, to begin with, that *depend* patterns with the prepositional phrase introduced by *for*, whereas *rely* patterns with the infinitive introduced by *to* (the "marked" infinitive). Thus, (1) "Rose depended on Jim for assistance in her political campaign," (2) "Rose relied on Jim to assist her in her political campaign," (3) "I'm depending on Jim for moral support," and (4) "I'm relying on Jim to lend moral support." It appears that *rely* recommends itself in sentences in which the expectation is for the person relied upon to physically *do* something, whereas *depend* is invoked when the expectation is that the person depended upon will *provide* something, something that need not involve physical activity. Consistent with this analysis is the fact that we rely on people, whereas we may depend on other things as well. Thus, "I rely on Jim to keep me informed about world affairs" but "I depend on my reading for information about world affairs." Although I think that the distinction as delineated here is a real one, I cannot think of a great deal of intuitive support for it; perhaps it is significant that a person who is self-reliant is able to do things for himself or herself, whereas a person who is independent requires no assistance of any kind.

deprecate/depreciate: although the meanings of these two words are beginning to coalesce in certain contexts, there remain contexts that require exclusively one or the other. The nonoverlapping meaning of *deprecate* is "to express disapproval of"; with this meaning compare the meaning of *depreciate*, "to assign a lower value to." Thus, compare the following sentences (1) "The hostess deprecated the table manners of her guests" and (2) "The Board of Overseers deprecated the custom practiced by many lawyers of billing clients by the page" with (3) "Martin tried to depreciate the importance of Flora's last remark" and (4) "Harry found it necessary to depreciate the value of Roger's contribution." The meaning of *depreciate* in (3) and (4) is of a piece with the meaning it has when used with words denoting monetary values like currency or credit: "The rise in value of the

British pound in the last several months has served to depreciate the value of the dollar."

detest/despise: both words mean "to dislike intensely," but the meaning of *despise* also comports an additional element, one of contempt or loathing. One would tend to detest someone for behavior, despise someone for character. Compare (1) "Various things that Harry did around the office irritated me; I learned to detest him" and (2) "I found Harry's treatment of his wife and children hateful; I grew to despise him."

dialectal/dialectical: the former of these words is derived from *dialect*, the latter from *dialectic*. A dialect is a variety of speech determined by a speaker's geographical origins or social class, whereas dialectic is the name given to a form of reasoning or argumentation that focuses on the resolution of contradictions. Thus, a form of speech determined by the speaker's region or social status is a dialectal—not a dialectical—variant, and the conduct of an argument that responded to the presence of contradictions would be characterized as dialectical, not dialectal.

dieresis (also diaeresis): a mark (¨) placed over the second of two identical vowels to indicate that they are to be treated as two separate sounds. Its use today is not mandatory, but its effect is frequently encountered in words like *deemphasize, reelect, zoology,* and *cooperate.*

different from/than: when the comparison is syntactically asymmetrical, as in "This problem is different from anything we have previously encountered," "His attitude was different from what I expected," then *from* is used. Consider now cases where the comparison is between elements that are syntactically symmetrical: (1) "This problem is different from the one (problem) we solved yesterday," (2) "This is a different problem than the one (problem) we solved yesterday," (3) "I saw in him an actor different from any (actor) I had ever seen before," and (4) "I saw in him a different actor than the one (actor) I had seen yesterday." In these sentences the choice between *from* and *than* seems to turn on whether the noun being compared precedes or follows *different*; when it precedes (1, 3), then *from* is used, when it follows (2, 4), then *than* is used. The explanation for this difference seems to be that in sentences structured like (2) and (4), in which the compared nouns follow *different*, the comparison appears to function as it does in an ordinary comparative construction ("This is a greater challenge than the one posed by unemployment," "This is a taller tree than that one."). However, when the noun being compared precedes *different*, as in (1) and (3), then the characteristic function of *different*, that of separating or dividing the compared elements, is rendered paramount and the *from* that renders this function is used.

dilemma/problem: following is an announcement made by a leading manufacturer of pharmaceutical products: "Our main dilemma is how to replace maturing products." This is another example of "striving" dialect, a variety of language in which a speaker is at pains to confer a tone of "elevation" upon the language used. One form taken in this attempt is to replace the word that would normally occur in a given position and substitute for it a word less commonly used; when the replacing word simply calls attention to itself, however, without adding to the discourse anything in the way of style or substance, then the substitution stands revealed as a willful and perverse endeavor, and the attempt defeats itself. Thus, we have speakers saying "I suspect it will rain tomorrow" rather than "I think it will rain tomorrow"; "The president gave an extraordinarily effective speech last night" instead of "The president gave an extremely effective speech last night"; "I'm enormously fond of strawberries" instead of "I'm very fond of strawberries" (even "I'm awfully fond of strawberries" is preferable). Speakers should certainly try to raise the level of their speech. But this cannot be done on the cheap; like other desirable attainments, a command of one's language requires study and application.

Returning now to our example, it is clear that the word that should obviously have been used in the context is *problem*. The word *dilemma* apparently recommended itself as appearing less prosaic and therefore to be preferred. But *dilemma* has a technical sense, knowledge of which would have ruled out its being used in the present context. A dilemma is a specific type of problem, one that presents a person with two equally balanced courses of action, the selection of either one usually entailing unwanted consequences. A person who was forced to choose between two houses similar in most respects, one of which had a faulty heating system but the other of which had a leaky roof, would be in a dilemma—or, as the idiom goes, be on the horns of a dilemma; similarly, someone accepted at two graduate schools, one of which had offered a full scholarship but the other of which had a better faculty in that student's field of specialization, would be in, or be facing, a dilemma. In our sample sentence, no such alternatively balanced situation faces the speaker. Therefore, the use of *dilemma* in that sentence—another instance of lexical overkill—is semantically disconcerting.

diminishment/diminution: although *diminution* would appear to be the noun formed from *diminish* and although the form *diminishment* does not receive a mention in some dictionaries, there is good reason to promote the latter form. The reason is that *diminution* suffers a form of semantic contamination from its morphological resemblance to the adjective *diminutive*. Frequently, when the occasion arises for the use of the nominal form, we wish merely to suggest that a reduction or lessening has taken place, without the further implication that the reduction or lessening is so drastic that the resulting product is tiny or minuscule. But use of *diminution* has this consequence. Consider a sentence such as "After Howard Patt had presented his arguments, there was a diminution of interest in the plan"; intended here is that the interest in the plan had been reduced—but not to the point where it was diminutive; *diminishment* would thus be preferable. Or consider the following two sentences: (1) "There was a marked diminishment of the sound that came from the adjoining room," and (2) "There was a marked diminution of the sound that came from the adjoining room." In (1), it appears that it is the volume of the sound coming into the neighboring room that is being assessed; in (2), it is the volume of the sound at its source—in the adjoining room—that is being assessed. Emily Dickinson concluded one of her poems, "[It's] by trades the size of these we men and women die." Although the consequences of trading in meaning are not nearly so fateful, it behooves us to mind what we say—others do.

disclose/divulge: both words mean "to reveal, make known, bring into the open," but associated with the word *divulge* is the sense that there is about what is divulged something secret or private, something based on a first-hand knowledge and thus known to but a limited number of people. If someone should say that the identity of a murderer, say, was disclosed by a reporter on the radio, it is a fair inference that the murderer's identity was made known, that is, divulged, to the reporter by someone who was directly involved with the murderer. Compare (1) "After months of speculation, the source of the leak was finally disclosed" and (2) "After months of speculation, the name of the leaker was finally divulged." (1) is consistent with the disclosure's having been made by an impersonal agency—a reporter or other type of news source, say, whereas (2) implies that the divulgence was made by someone who was in close connection with the person who actually did the leaking.

disregard/ignore: examine the following sentence: "In voting to extend the session for another day, the members of the committee ignored their own rule." Why does *ignore* seem to be the wrong word here? It appears that *ignore* is properly used of things that are present in our surroundings; thus, a person's presence, an oncoming car, a verbal command, a swarm of bees, and so on are things that we may choose to ignore. But if we pay no attention to things like rules, conventions, stipulations, contracts, and the like—things, that is, that are not present to our immediate awareness—such things are not ignored, they are disregarded. For a thing to be ignored, we have to be aware of its presence; if the thing is such, however, that we are merely aware of its existence, then if we fail to take notice of it we do not ignore it, we disregard it.

distracted/distraught/distrait: by its form, *distracted* may represent either an adjective or a past participle: We may use it adjectivally as when we say "Donald was distracted when Rhea asked him whether he had turned off the gas," intending the meaning that Donald was in a state of distraction when Rhea questioned him (not that Rhea's question distracted him), or we may use the word in a sentence like "Donald was distracted by the sound of gunfire outside his house," in which case *distracted* is functioning as a past participle. In its participial use, the word means something like "having one's attention diverted." In its adjectival use it means "being in a state of inattentiveness from one's attention being directed elsewhere." The word *distraught* is an adjective, and it means "being in a state of bewilderment or confusion from having had one's attention diverted." The difference in meaning between (a) *distracted* (adjective) and (b) *distraught* is thus that with (a) the diversion of attention is a function of the principal involved, whereas in (b) the diversion is caused by factors apart from the principal. The word *distrait*, finally, means "being inattentive because of an anxiety caused by having been distracted by worries, concerns, fears, and so on." The difference in meaning between (b) *distraught* and (c) *distrait* is that with (b) the emphasis is on the state of confusion caused by the distraction, whereas with (c) it is on the anxiety that results from the discovery that one is in such a state.

dived/dove: these present-day alternatives of the past tense derive from an interesting set of circumstances. In Old English (Anglo-Saxon), certain verb forms were paired in the sense that one was intransitive, the other a causative. This relation is maintained in

Modern English between pairs like *sit/set, lie/lay, rise/raise, drink/drench, fall/fell,* and others: to set something down, for example, is to cause it to sit, to fell a tree is to cause it to fall, and so on. In Old English this type of relation obtained between the verbs *dūfan and dȳfan,* the former meaning "to sink," the latter "to immerse," that is, "cause to sink." Further, *dūfan* was a strong verb in Old English, *dȳfan,* was weak. Our present-day *dived* is thus a continuation of the weak preterit (past tense) *dȳfde,* whereas *dove* is a development (somewhat irregular) from the Old English past tense form *dēaf.* Either form is correct.

divers/diverse: although the two words have a common etymon, ultimately, a Latin verb meaning "to turn away from," they have developed slightly (but definitely) different meanings. *Divers* has the meaning "several, many, various," *diverse* the meaning "different, unlike, variegated." In the following sentences, cross-substitution of our two words would render the explanatory subordinate clauses largely inapposite and would produce, in consequence, ungainly semantic structures: (1) "Every incoming president must be prepared to deal with divers appeals, as each individual constituency enters a plea for its own cause" and (2) "Every incoming president must be prepared to deal with diverse appeals, some coming from constituencies of the left, some from those of the right." The two words differ also in their pronunciations, *divers* being stressed on the first syllable and ending with a *z* sound, and *diverse* being stressed on the second syllable and ending with an *s* sound.

dose/dosage: a dose is a quantity taken at one time; a dosage is an amount prescribed for a given period of time. Thus, a patient's daily dosage of aspirin could be four tablets, two taken in the morning and two in the evening; two tablets would then constitute a dose. A doctor might reduce the dosage of a given medicine for a patient from four to three doses a day. To be avoided is a usage like the following: "Last night, before going to bed, I took a large dosage of castor oil."

doubt that/if: when *doubt* takes a clause as its object, the proper complementizer is *that*, not *if*. Thus, "I doubt that he solved the problem" is correct. The word *if*, however, does not function to make an object complement of the clause that it initiates; its primary function, rather, is that of a conjunction introducing a dependent clause. In general, such a clause may occur before or after the main clause with which it is in construction. Therefore, in a sentence like "I doubt if he solved the problem," there echoes dissonantly in the syntactic background the sentence "If he solved the problem, (then) I doubt," or, spelled out, "Either he solved the problem, or he didn't. If he did, then I (am in) doubt."

doubtful/dubious: although these two terms are used more-or-less interchangeably—to describe either a person's state of mind or a characteristic of a state of affairs—there is some basis for restricting *doubtful* to the former use. One hears both "I'm dubious about that proposition" and (2) "That's a dubious proposition," both (3) "I'm doubtful about that proposition" and (4) "That's a doubtful proposition." I'm a little dubious about (4), however; it seems to me doubtful that (4) is as precisely worded a proposition as is (2). The background for this response is probably something like the following: one of the major functions of the suffix *-ful* is to derive adjectives from a class of nouns like *hope, remorse, resent, deceit, glee,* and the like, a class whose members have meanings referring to human feelings and affections. Thus, in a sentence like (4) there is, because of this derivational background, a perverse intimation that a proposition is entertaining a doubt. The point seems to be that a person is capable of doubting, whereas a thing is dubitable, may be doubted. A further consideration is that *dubious*, unlike *doubtful*, carries with it the connotation of suspicion.

duplicate/replicate: a distinction may be drawn between these two words on the basis that *replicate* is derived from *replica*, whose meaning properly connotes "a copy—of a concrete object or of an objective representation," whereas *duplicate* conveys a more general sense of "to produce again" or "to reproduce"; in other words, duplication may be regarded as an activity because one duplicates something, but replication is a process in which something is replicated. We might contrast, say, (1) "Houses of this design are replicated in many communities" and (2) "It would be hard to duplicate in another setting the charm communicated by this house." There is a tendency to overuse *replicate*; thus, although its use would be questionable in a sentence like (2), that sort of use is frequently encountered. The following sentence, recently encountered, illustrates this overuse: (3) "Other writers will undoubtedly try to replicate Barry's success." Why the deviation from the expected? Why, indeed.

economic/economical: recently, a speaker, in the course of recommending a certain proposal for improving the financial condition of a local municipality, declared: (1) "This is a sound economical plan." As here stated, the plan is being recommended not so much as one that it would be advantageous for the municipality to adopt (a representation that it was clearly the intention of the speaker to make) as it is to represent the plan as one that would not cost much (or, alternatively, as one that was not lengthy in its expression). The meaning of the word *economic* that is relevant in the present context is "pertaining to the production and use of income"; the meaning of *economical* is "avoiding waste, being careful of resources." In fact, as (1) stands, it would require a comma between *sound* and *economical*—to indicate that *plan* is being modified by both *sound* and *economical*; whereas in the correct version (2) "This is a sound economic plan," no comma would be indicated, inasmuch as *sound* is here modifying *economic plan*.

efficiency/efficacy: the meanings of both words contain a component that evaluates success in the carrying out of a project or in the performance of a task; *efficiency* assigns this valuation to the task as it is being performed, *efficacy* assigns it to the task in relation to its completion. If we compare (1) "Lucy did her work with great efficiency" and (2) "Lucy did her work with great efficacy," we infer from (1) that Lucy's work was competent, but from (2) that it was successful. It is a greater compliment to say of Lucy that she was an efficacious worker than to say that she was (merely) an efficient worker.

egotistic/egotistical: in the following sentence, the two adjectives are in the proper form: "For me to describe for you my amatory triumphs would be egotistic, and since I'm not an egotistical person, you'll have to excuse me." It appears that the *-ic* suffix, when added to nouns like *egotist, casuist, anarchist, theist, sadist,* and the like—that is, to nouns formed with the agent suffix *-ist*—derives an adjective that describes the type of activity that would be engaged in by the type of person referred to by the underlying form: Thus, an egotist says egotistic things, a theist thinks theistic thoughts, a casuist argues with casuistic reasoning, an anarchist makes anarchistic speeches, a sadist employs sadistic practices, and so on. When to these *-istic* forms there is added, in turn, the suffix *-al,* a new adjectival form is derived, one, this time, that describes the mental tendency, disposition, or orientation of the type of person referred to by the underlying noun. Therefore, a casuist has a casuistical temperament, a theist embraces a theistical religious doctrine, a sadist observes a sadistical moral practice, and so forth.

elder (eldest): *elder* and *eldest* are the original comparative and superlative degrees of *old.* The variation in vowel quality between *old* and *elder (eldest)* derives from the presence originally of an element (*i*) that caused "umlaut," or mutation of the vowel in the preceding syllable. Accordingly, forms roughly of the following structure—*old, oldis, oldisto*—would, by developments too intricate to spell out here, result in *old, elder, eldest.* The forms *older, oldest* were later, analogical developments. The *e* forms are today used primarily in the context of describing priority in the order of family offspring; one speaks of an elder or eldest son or daughter. From this standpoint the eldest might be a son or daughter who died in infancy and was succeeded by several more children. The *o* forms, on the contrary, are used in cases where an actual comparison is being made. On this score, one of several living children would be the oldest even though he or she was preceded by an "eldest" child who had earlier died. In referring to one of her two sons, a mother might say "John is my elder son," but if she were comparing his age with that of her other son, she would say "John is my older son." In other words, the *e* forms are used when precedence with respect to birth is the point at issue, the *o* forms when the point is seniority with respect to age. When what is being discussed is the comparative ages of buildings, cars, houses, and other such inanimate things, the form, of course, is *older*.

elusive/evasive: both words mean "to avoid, to slip away"; in general, however, *elusive* is used when what is being avoided is physical capture or apprehension, whereas *evasive* is used when what is being avoided is direct or relevant response to a verbal challenge. One is therefore elusive with respect to one's person but evasive with respect to one's answers. By this criterion, animals can be elusive but not evasive. Although both words can occur in the same environment, the inferences would be different: "Seymour is an elusive person" would mean that he is hard to pin down as to his whereabouts; "Seymour is an evasive person" would mean that he is hard to pin down as to his convictions.

emigrate/immigrate: one emigrates from (out of) a country and immigrates to a country. Thus, an emigrant is a person leaving a country, an immigrant an arrival into a country. The same person may be looked upon now as an emigrant, say from Australia, and as an immigrant from Australia; the difference is one of orientation: The person is an emigrant from the standpoint of previous departure from Australia, an immigrant from the standpoint of current residency in the United States.

enhance/increase: a spokesman for a government agency, speaking of the lack of oversight in its previous management, put it this way: (1) "It's like a car without headlights. It doesn't mean it's going to go off the road, but it enhances your chances of not making the next curve." What is there about this sentence that occasions a second take? Consider that *increase* means "to make greater," *enhance* means "to raise to a higher degree" and is used as a rule when the raising has the consequence of benefiting someone or improving the status of something—so that, in effect, its meaning is "to improve, or to make better." One would say "His chances for success in his profession were enhanced when he took the course in accounting" but "His chances for failure in his profession were increased when he decided to spend his time playing pinball machines." Why not then the obvious "increases" in (1)? There is a strong temptation in using the language to "make it new," a practice that when properly motivated and controlled—when the principle amounts actually to "making it new, and better"—may indeed lead to felicitous results. To achieve such results, however, the novel formulation must say what the replaced formulation said and then some, the "then some" residing in the way what is said is expressed. In (1), however, we have the replacement of the expected word without the justifying supplement; in other words, we have simply newness for its own sake—I should say, rather, newness for ego's sake.

entreat/beseech: the shared component of meaning is something like "to ask for, to petition, to make an appeal," but *beseech* is used when the request has a greater sense of urgency. Thus, the following might be sentences used by a mother to a son: (1) "I entreat you to drive more carefully" and (2) "I beseech you to stop using drugs." Roughly synonymous with *beseech* in (2) would be *beg*, with its sense of abject supplication, whereas substituting that word in (1) would not produce near-synonymy but would, instead, significantly strengthen the intensity of the request.

envision/envisage: both forms have the general meaning "to project a mental picture of some sort," but with *envision* that picture may be more abstract. The difference in the degree of distinctness derives from the respective natures of the two words to which the *en* is prefixed, that is, *visage* refers to an image that is delineated, whereas *vision* can be used to refer to an appearance that is indefinite or immaterial. Compare "In her calculations, she envisaged herself as the head of the corporation" and "In her daydreams, she envisioned a future full of contentment and well-being." Interchange of the verbs in these two sentences would produce a tinge of inappropriateness.

envy/jealousy: although there is a considerable overlap in the meanings of these two words, there appears to be a basis for distinguishing between them in the sense that *jealousy* is reflective of a principal's feelings or attitudes toward another person, whereas *envy* expresses a principal's feelings or attitudes toward another person's advantages or accomplishments. In certain contexts it makes little difference whether we use one or the other of the two forms. We may say both (1) "I envy Wilmer" ("I'm envious of Wilmer") and (2) "I'm jealous of Wilmer"; more fully, either (3) "I envy Wilmer his education" or (4) "I'm jealous of Wilmer's education." (Even in these rudimentary contexts, one may sense a frisson of the semantic difference suggested here; thus, (1) evokes the question of why, for what reason, Wilmer is envied, whereas (2) is self-sufficient.) In those contexts where the focus is squarely on the feelings experienced by the speaker, there is a use that is peculiar to *jealous*. Compare (5) "Wilmer was jealous of Harriet's continued affection," where *jealous* has the meaning of "watchful" and (6) "Wilmer was jealous of his remaining resources," where *jealous* means "protective." A sentence like (7) "Wilmer was jealous of his wife's affectionate glances" can therefore be taken as ambiguous. It could mean that the glances were directed at Wilmer, that he watched for them and prized them, as in (5), or it could mean that the glances were directed at others and that Wilmer, feeling proprietorial about them, resented their untoward expenditure, a reading like that of (6).

epigram/epigraph: an epigram is a short statement that makes an interesting, frequently a profound, observation about life or the world; an epigraph, too, is a statement, though one culled from the writings or sayings of someone else and used as the heading for a chapter in a book. Thus, there is no reason that someone's epigram cannot be used by someone else as an epigraph. In general, however, epigraphs are not thus restricted; any sentiment, no matter what its source, as long as it expresses what an author deems appropriate to the purpose, may be mustered to serve as an epigraph.

estimate/estimation: compare (1) "By (According to) my estimate, the project will be completed in two years" and (2) "In my estimation, this project has been mismanaged from the outset." Exchange of our two nouns in these contexts would cause both sentences to resound somewhat dissonantly. The reason for this probably lies along the following lines: The noun *estimate* implies that a calculation has been performed and that it is on the basis of that calculation that a judgment or valuation is being proffered; *estimation*, by contrast, implies that an on-the-spot evaluation is being performed and that what is being rendered is an opinion based on that evaluation. An estimate, in other words, conveys a more reasoned and more impersonal judgment than does an estimation.

This difference in semantic nuance probably stems from the different derivational backgrounds of the two words. The noun *estimate*, formed by conversion from the verb of the same form, carries along in its meaning the verb's sense of computing, of calculating; *estimation*, though, is derived from the verb *esteem* and has apparently modulated that verb's sense of judging, a meaning still displayed in such uses as "I esteem him worthy of the honor," into the somewhat weaker sense of mere opinion.

euphemism: a "good-speaking" substitute for another word that, for reasons of tact or delicacy, the speaker (or writer) thinks should be avoided. Why, for example, are "undertakers" so called? Because, we might say, they take people under. But in taking people under, what in fact do they do? Why, they bury them, of course. *Undertaker* is a euphemism for *burier*—just as *inter* is a euphemism for *bury*, and as *place of interment* is a euphemism for *cemetery*, itself a euphemism for *graveyard*. Euphemisms are usually substituted for words that describe events or functions that are associated with the less agreeable aspects of our existence: words associated with death, bodily functions, lowly trades, and the like.

A slightly different type of substitution, but one that, like euphemism, is motivated by a wish to avoid the connotations that are associated with the words that would normally be used for the purpose, is effected by a substitute that we might call an *apophemism*, that is, a "side-speaking" device; here, what is being bypassed or left aside are certain negative associations connected with the normally occurring word. Consider "frosted flakes"; what is being avoided (and implicitly being papered over) by this description? Well, that what the flakes are "frosted" with is sugar. Or consider "gaming casinos," places where gambling is the only game in sight; or consider the lingo of the stock markets, in which stocks may go up, but never down. Instead, stocks experiencing the latter inglorious fate are said to be "off," an utterance that, in the mouths of certain commentators sounds very much like "up," serving thus to strike momentary terror in the hearts of dialect-insensitive short-traders.

eventually/ultimately: *eventually* means "finally, at a future point in time"; *ultimately* means "last, final, or furthest in some projected scheme or time frame." Of the two forms, *eventually* is more closely allied to the idea of occurrence in the future. Thus, if we compare (1) "Barry will eventually pass the bar exam" and

(2) "Barry will ultimately pass the bar exam," the meaning in (1) is that he will pass the exam at some future date, whereas (2) might be used to stress the fact that the applicant will in the course of events be successful. Moreover, unlike *eventually*, *ultimately* can be used to refer to a time that is not in the future, say a time that is regarded as the past from some future point of view. Thus, one can say "Ultimately, this project will have been finished." If one used *eventually* in a construction like this, as in "Eventually this project will have been finished," a certain dissonance would be registered between the use of the future perfect aspect of the verb—conveying the sense that the action had been completed—and the sense implicit in *eventually* that projects the action into some future time, thus that it remains to be completed.

exceptional/exceptionable: *exceptional* means "what exceeds, is an exception to, the ordinary or the expected"; *exceptionable* means "something of which exception might be made or to which exception might be taken, which might be rejected, or objected to." Compare (1) "There was nothing exceptional in the contract" and (2) "There was nothing exceptionable in the contract." (1) suggests that the contract was more or less routine, containing nothing unexpected; (2) does not expressly make that comment (the contract may, in fact, not be routine), but the examiner feels no need to challenge any part of it.

expense/expenditure: *expenditure* refers to an actual outlay of money or goods, whereas *expense* has a more general sense, that of a charge or cost for the procurement of goods or the maintenance of property; we might say that we have expenses, but we make expenditures. Compare (1) "Among my expenses are those for books and food" and (2) "Among my expenditures are those for books and food." Sentence (1) simply expresses the fact that books and food are causes or occasions for the expenditure of funds, but it does not imply that funds have actually been expended, whereas (2) refers to the actual outlay of funds for those items.

explain/explicate: *explain* means "to give an account of something so as to make it clear or understandable"; *explicate* means essentially the same thing, but its meaning also contains the implication that the something of which an account is being given is more complicated and that the account is more detailed and, perhaps, more logically constructed. Because of its less restricted sense, *explain* is used in a wider variety of connections than is *explicate*: One may explain why one has a headache, why the dog is barking, or why a child is crying; in all such cases a single fact or reason is sufficient to provide the "explanation"; however, it would be explication that was called for when the account to be given is that of the meaning of a poem or the implications of a legal document, in which cases it would be a question of constructing a consistent account of the sentences or clauses in the respective documents.

extraordinarily: this is a highly overused adverbial modifier: there is little semantic warrant for uses like "He was extraordinarily heavy," "This is an extraordinarily inexpensive stock," "Her debut was extraordinarily successful." Its occurrence does not stand out so much in the speech of British speakers, who manage to pronounce it in a slurrage of three syllables, but in the speech of Americans, who allot to the word its full complement of (seven) syllables, the motivation for its use seems to be largely the wish to elongate speaking time. In 98 percent of its uses the actual sense would be more appropriately rendered by a word like *extremely* or *exceedingly*—not to mention the always serviceable *very*.

factitious/fictitious: both adjectives contain a semantic component having the sense of "made up, contrived." In *factitious*, this sense is opposed to what is genuine; in *fictitious*, the sense is opposed to that which is real. A factitious enthusiasm, say, would be an artificial, a dissembled enthusiasm, but it is not clear that there could be a fictitious enthusiasm. This is because enthusiasm can be faked, but it cannot be invented. A factitious story might be one designed to serve some purpose, to meet some contingency; such a story, one might say, is concocted; however, a fictitious story would be one whose primary purpose was to deceive; such a story is fabricated. A fictitious story, it should be noted, is not the same as a fictional story; with the latter there is no intent to deceive, and the story is imagined and composed.

(the) fact of the matter: in the great majority of cases, *the fact is* is all that is required. *The fact of the matter* is properly used when one of the participants in a discussion decides that the comments have been aimless or irrelevant, at which point—to focus the discussion on the matter at hand—the person may say, "Actually, the fact of the matter is . . ." This function of the phrase is heavily exploited in current political discussions, where Democrats and Republicans, striving continually to "spin" an issue to their political advantage, use it to focus or refocus the discussion so that it reflects their partisan interests. In such discussions the phrase takes on an almost ritual significance. In general, however, it is the penchant of many politicians for verbal amplitude that encourages use of the phrase when simply *the fact is* would suffice. (This particular verbal virus has spread, so that we now have, as another example of syntactic vacuity, "the truth of the matter.")

falsity/falsehood: truth and falsity are functions of the relation that holds between a statement and the facts or the state of affairs that the statement purports to describe. If the relation is one of correspondence, then the statement is true; if it is one of noncorrespondence, then the statement is false. Furthermore, a statement of which this correspondence holds is a truth; one of which it does not hold is a falsehood. We therefore say a statement is true but that it is or that it expresses a truth: "Bears are omnivores" is true, and the claim that bears are omnivores expresses a truth.

Similarly, "Bears are not omnivores" is false, and the claim that bears are not omnivores is a falsehood. We say that a statement is false, but that it is or that it expresses a falsehood. When we say that a statement is false, we say it on the basis of our own, differing, assessment of the relation between the statement and facts in the world; when we say that a statement is a falsehood, we say it because we harbor some doubt or skepticism about the speaker's reason or justification for making the claim. A lie differs from a falsehood in that a lie is produced with full knowledge of the non-correspondence between the claim made by the statement and the facts—in other words, with full knowledge that the statement is false. When we charge somebody with telling a lie, we are making our own assessment of the relation that is claimed in the statement; when we charge somebody with uttering a falsehood, we are implying a reservation about the speaker's qualifications, intention, or motive in making the statement.

farther/further: of the two forms, *farther* is generally preferred when the context is that of distance—in space or time; thus, "Mars is farther from the earth than is Venus," "I ran farther that day than I ever had run before," "The French Revolution took place farther back in time than did the Civil War." *Further* is less preferred in these contexts but is used in a variety of others, namely: "He made a further point, this one about the proper way to bunt," "I submit this plan for your further consideration," "I have nothing further to say about this topic."

fearful/fearsome: basically, the difference is that someone may be fearful, someone or something may be fearsome. Thus, we may say "Mt. Everest is a fearsome mountain" but either "Bill is a fearsome mountaineer" or "Bill is a fearful mountaineer."

feel bad/feel badly: *feel* is a verb that may be used to refer to our sense of touch or to describe a dispositional state. Groping about in the dark for a light switch and having little success, one might say "(My), I'm feeling badly"; or, if in general one has difficulty in recognizing forms by touch, one might say "I feel badly," indicating by so saying that this shortcoming is habitual. If, on the other hand, one is feeling depressed or dyspeptic, the proper way to describe that mental or physical condition is by saying "I'm feeling bad" or "I feel bad." We might notice that to express the corresponding positive physical state, we say "I'm feeling good" or "I feel good" (the version "I feel well" is by now well-enough established to be used more-or-less synonymously with "I feel good"). On the other hand, there is something deplorable about uses like "Seymour feels (or "felt") badly about how he conducted himself the other night."

finally/lastly: the basic distinction is that *finally* is the form to be used when the item being introduced therewith figures as part of a process or development, whereas *lastly* should be used when the item being introduced counts as part of a list. Compare the following sentences: (1) "Finally, the last brick has been laid in the west wall" and (2) "Lastly, I wish to thank my colleagues for their support." Sentence (1) might be uttered by a building foreman at the conclusion of a construction job, (2) in the preface to a book, closing a recitation of acknowledgments.

flabbergasted/nonplussed: consider a TV talk show in which two commentators, each representing an opposite position on the political spectrum, discuss current political issues. In the sign-off at the end of a typical discussion, Commentator A turns to Commentator B and says, (1) "You know, B, your comments tonight make me ashamed to be on the same program with you." On hearing this comment at the end of a program that from his point of view was in no way out of the ordinary, B's face assumes an astonished (aghast) expression and he either makes no reply or he utters a startled "What!"—he is flabbergasted. At the end of another program, A signs off with (2) "No matter how hard you try, B, you cannot conceal your ultraliberal views." B, who thought he was on this occasion taking particular pains to be objective, has now on his face a look of exceeding puzzlement and manages to say merely, "Please!"—he is nonplussed. In both cases the reaction is against an assertion that was totally unexpected. In case (1), the assertion was so entirely unrelated to anything he had said that B could not imagine what possible form his reply might take; in case (2), the assertion ran so directly counter to B's intention, he having tried throughout the discussion to convey precisely the opposite impression, that there was nothing more (*non plus*) that he could think of to add.

flaunt/flout: one flaunts (makes much of) something of one's own—one's wealth, good looks, education; one flouts (disregards or violates) something outside oneself—a law, a regulation, a convention. Thus, we may say "Almost every time Darren spoke, he flaunted the fact that he had attended Princeton University"; "In whatever city Darren found himself, he was sure to flout one or another of its traffic regulations." Occasionally, these words are interchanged; the result, of course, being solecistic—as it is in the following passage occurring in a TV documentary: "Germany was at that time subject to the Treaty of Versailles, but Hitler decided to flaunt the treaty."

folk etymology: the name given to a process whereby a word whose meaning is not clearly reflected in its form is refashioned so as to achieve such correspondence. The process implicates a new etymology for the word, but since the implicated etymology has no historical warrant, is motivated by a fancied but totally inapposite connection, the process is referred to as "folk etymology." There are, basically, two ways in which the process operates: In one, the authentic word presents itself as semantically opaque and is reconstituted by the speaker into a form with elements whose meanings are "transparent" and that preserve something of the original meaning; thus, the Spanish *cucaracha* ("wood louse") has been morphologically transmogrified to *cockroach*; in the process the meaning of the word has been rendered more "accessible." Similar in some ways is an example that occurs in *David Copperfield*, where Miss Mowcher exclaims, on taking her leave from Steerforth and David: "'Bob swore,' as the Englishman said for 'Good night,' when he first learnt French and thought it so like English. 'Bob swore,' my ducks." To cite another example: The etymologically correct *shamefast* is replaced by *shamefaced*, a form whose composite meaning more clearly describes the attitude of open contrition that the word is used to represent; compare also *helpmate*.

In the second process, the substitution is not so much concerned with preservation of meaning as with preservation of reference. In this type, the challenging form is replaced by a word that resembles it phonetically but whose meaning, while known to the speaker, has nothing to do with the meaning of the original word; thus, varicose veins may be referred to as "various" veins, a traverse rod is referred to as a "traveler's" rod, and so on. Someone referring to the departure of an angry man from a meeting described the man as leaving "in a state of high dungeon." A rather striking example occurred recently on a TV talk show. During a discussion of reported UFO sightings, one of the participants remarked that there had been an increase recently in "extratorrential" activity. Here might be mentioned also the report of a traveler to Russia who, on returning to the United States, specified as one of the peculiar traits of the Russians their use of the "acrylic" alphabet.

Folk etymologies, as revisions of the customary, expected forms that they replace, somewhat resemble in the general scheme of usage the type of replacement I have spent so much time criticizing in these pages. Whether one says "This is a gem of the first order," not comprehending the significance of and thus misrendering "gem of the first water" or says "I have a simplistic plan that will solve all your problems," bypassing the expected "simple" for the purpose of sounding more sophisticated, an extension has been made of the language's expressive potential. The resemblance is quite superficial, however (in fact, I have strained to make it): Cases of folk etymology require simple correction; cases of verbal pushiness merit censure.

for him and I (and similar constructions): nouns or pronouns occurring after prepositions must be inflected in the accusative case. In English, of course, nouns do not have a special inflected form for the accusative case, so that no selection is necessary when they are in the accusative. But a number of pronouns do have special accusative forms, and it is a common error to use the nominative when the accusative form is required. No one would say "I gave the book to he" or "He was looking for I," but when these pronominal forms occur in conjunction with another pronoun (particularly with *you*, which does not have a distinctive accusative form), errors are commonly heard. Compare "Ben said that he often thought about her and I," "I bought the book for you and he," "Ben said that the invitation was for you and I." In all these sentences the second pronoun should be in the accusative case, rendered as *me, him, me,* respectively. The same error occurs, of course, when the first member of the conjunction is a name or other type of noun phrase; thus, we have the incorrect "Ben said the present was for Mary and I" and "He said the present was for my brother and I." In the same way, it is an error to use the nominative pronominal form when the pronoun is the direct object of the verb, another construction that requires the accusative case. Thus, the following constructions are incorrect (not merely inappropriate): "Don invited her and I to the party," "Don told Alfred and I what happened." These usages are not merely transgressions against proper usage; they violate the rules of English grammar; as such, they should be more assiduously guarded against.

forcefully/forcibly: the element of force is present in both words, but *forcibly* connotes physical force, whereas the force suggested by *forcefully* need not be physical and can in fact be of any nature aimed at producing a desired effect. One can therefore say that a politician argued forcefully or lobbied forcefully for passage of a certain bill. *Forcibly*, however, might be used in constructions like "He pushed the door in forcibly" and "The men were at work forcibly prying the two trucks apart." Consider the contrast also in the adjectival pair *forceful/forcible*: (1) "Kramer made a forceful entrance" and (2) "Kramer made a forcible entry." Sentence (1) describes a situation where Kramer projected force, (2) where he used force.

founder/flounder: following is a sentence recently encountered: (1) "The district attorney first argued that Mr. _____ had been guilty of extortion, and when this case floundered in 1989, he switched to the fraudulent-bankruptcy argument." It is pretty clear that the word the author should have used in (1) is *founder*, in its sense of "to break down, to collapse." Of course, *flounder*, with its sense of "to stumble about, to proceed clumsily," has just enough relevance to the case at hand that it may not be irrefutably ruled out. But whereas the use of *flounder* in (1) raises some question as to its propriety, *founder* in that context would be acceptable without any question.

frantic/frenetic: dictionaries define *frantic* as something along the lines of "wild or extremely agitated by reason of fear, anxiety, worry, or passion" and then give for *frenetic* the definition "frantic" (for both words, *frenzied* is given as a synonym). Consider now the sentences (1) "Desmond was frantic with fear" and (2) "Desmond's actions were frenetic." If the two adjectives were exchanged in these two sentences, the semantic fit would not be as good. The reason for this effect is that the meaning of *frantic* pertains to a mental state or condition, to a frame of mind, whereas that of *frenetic* pertains rather to a type of behavior or conduct. (Cf., as analogous, "He's worried" and "He's delirious.") It is for this reason that *frenetically* is more apt as an adverbial form than is *frantically*. In a sentence like (3) "Desmond waved his arms frantically," the semantic focus, despite the adverb, falls on Desmond; we think that in his frantic state, he was waving his arms, whereas in (4) "Desmond waved his arms frenetically," the focus falls on the way Desmond waved his arms; we think, he was gesticulating wildly.

free variation: in the matter of pronunciation it is not always the case that there is one and only one correct way to pronounce a given word. Words like *advertisement, either, neither, insurance, radiator, garage, route,* and a good many others are pronounced by some speakers consistently in one way and by others equally consistently another way. Although some inference may sometimes be drawn about the speaker's age, dialectal region, or level of education from such preferences, there is no basis for concluding that one pronunciation is correct and the other incorrect. The two pronunciations are said to "vary freely," meaning that neither one is to be proscribed as incorrect.

frugal/thrifty: both words mean "practicing economy in the management of funds," but *frugal* refers more directly to practicing that economy in the course of shopping for goods or services, whereas *thrifty* applies more to the preservation of funds. *Frugal* is more properly used in a context of spending, *thrifty* in a context of saving. A person whose income is limited could be frugal but in no position to exercise thrift, whereas a person with a generous income could be thrifty but under no necessity to exercise frugality.

functional shift: a process whereby a word belonging to one part of speech is employed as a different part of speech. Words like *fund* and *task*, for example, originally nouns, have been shifted from their original membership in the class of nouns and made to function as verbs: Compare "He was finally able to fund his project" and "I'm tasking you to carry out this project." This process, sometimes called *conversion*, is very productive in English; it may effect shifts between just about any parts of speech. Adjectives, for example, are easily made to undergo this process: Thus, we have "The meek shall inherit the earth," "Youth is wasted on the young," and so on. The process may even effect conversion from the status of intransitive to that of transitive verb; compare, for example, "We expect to grow the business at a rate of fifteen to twenty percent a year."

gantlet/gauntlet: in its specific meaning, *gantlet* refers to a section of railroad track at which two parallel pairs of tracks converge for a space into a single track and then again diverge; in its specific meaning, *gauntlet* refers to a type of glove with a protective cuff. Although to some extent the two terms may be used interchangeably, the specific meanings can be used to make nice distinctions in the common expressions (1) "run a gantlet" and (2) "fling down the gauntlet." That is, in expression (1) what the person runs is, like the railroad track gantlet, a narrow passage, formed in this case by two lines of individuals; in (2), the expression harks back to a time when dueling was common and a challenge was issued by flinging down a gauntlet, that is, a glove.

garner/garnish: *garner* means "to gather or acquire"; *garnish* means "to add something decorative or ornamental." One garners votes or testimonials but garnishes a ham or a cocktail. Occasionally, a mistake like the following is encountered: "People talked a lot about him in the press, and that garnished a lot of notoriety for him."

generality/generalization: in its standard sense, a generality is an indefinite, nonspecific statement or observation, one that describes a condition, situation, or set of facts *in general*. To speak in generalities is to speak about a subject broadly, omitting detail and substantiation. Thus, it is a generality to say of corporate executives that they are overpaid—some are and some are not. Likewise, it would be a generality to say that ballplayers lead carefree lives—some do and some do not. A generalization, by contrast, is a statement or conclusion inferred from a set of experiments, observations, or descriptions; being based upon data that are available for independent inspection, a generalization is more substantive, has more probative value, than does a generality. To speak now in generalities, a generality is an expression of someone's opinion that something is generally true; a generalization is a conclusion that finds that something holds generally of a set of data and that offers that finding as a generalization.

go slow: *slow* is one of a group of native adverbs whose derivational background (i.e., the formation of an adverb by adding to the underlying adjective a final -*e* [which was subsequently lost]) is such that there is no morphological difference between adjectival and adverbial forms. Included in this class are adverbs like *hard, fast, late* (cf. "Tubby McCool arrived late" and "Tubby McCool arrived early," i.e., prematurely), *clean* ("I clean forgot to repair the faucet"). Most of these so-called flat adverbs have developed variants with the -*ly* suffix whose use has largely superseded that of the flat variants; this is particularly the case where *slow* is concerned. The purpose of this article is simply to indicate that etymological background would provide a sanction for uses like "go slow" or "drive slow." Historical sanction, however, is probably not enough to justify perseverance in using these forms.

gourmet/gourmand: both words refer to people who are fond of eating (and drinking). A gourmet, however, has limited, refined gustatory tastes, whereas the taste of a gourmand is more encompassing. Where the gourmet is interested in dainty and exquisitely prepared morsels, the gourmand is concerned with being served a full measure. A gourmet will sniff a glass of wine before drinking it; a gourmand will, before drinking a beer, blow the suds off.

grandiloquence/magniloquence: some dictionaries treat these two words as having no appreciable difference in meaning. Both of course refer to a type of language that is above the ordinary in its character and in the effect that it produces. A distinction in their respective meanings can be drawn, however, in the respect that *magniloquence* refers to a language that is lofty or extravagant, whereas *grandiloquence* refers to a language that is pompous or bombastic. Thus, attribution of magniloquence to a speech or a speaker may be regarded as a compliment, whereas an attribution of grandiloquence might be taken as a criticism.

hanged/hung: either form is acceptable as the past tense of *hang*; the only point to be made in connection with these forms is that some speakers regard it as preferable when what is being described is the mortal dangle at the end of a rope to use the variant *hanged*: "The prisoner was hanged at midnight."

haplology: a term used to describe the loss of a syllable under the conditions of morphological combination. Thus, whereas the combining of *dialect* and the suffix *-ology* yields the expected *dialectology*, and the combining of *phrase* and *-ology* yields *phraseology*, the combining of *criminal* and *-ology* does not yield the expected *criminalology*, but instead *criminology*. The same (reductive) process is at work in a formation like *mineralogy*. Consider, further, forms like *animation, gravitation, isolation*. The suffix here is *-ation*, and we find it normally added in formations like *gradation, expectation, realization*, and so on (see even *formation*). But *animation*, and the rest, if not subjected to haplologization, would yield *animatation*. Similarly for *gravitation, isolation*, and other such forms.

heal/cure: fundamentally, the two words differ in that *heal* is an intransitive verb, whereas *cure* is transitive: Healing is a process in which an organism's health is restored; curing is a method that promotes healing. A person heals—of a wound, a disease, an illness. A treatment, instituted by a physician, cures a person of the wound, disease, or illness. From this point of view, it is not quite precise to say "My doctor (or "this treatment") healed me."

healthy/healthful: *healthy* is properly used as a (positive) description of a person's physical state (or of certain factors that pertain to that state), *healthful* of something that (favorably) affects that state. A person may therefore be called healthy, and a food, a product, an activity may be healthful (of course, we can also speak of a plant as being healthy and of mulch as being healthful for the plant). A person's appetite, as a factor pertaining to the physical state of that person, may be called "healthy," whereas a particular diet, if it in fact conduces to the person's good health, will be healthful. These strictures having been laid down, it must be conceded that no great breach of usage is entrained by saying, as is common, "Spinach is a healthy food" or "Milk is healthy for you."

historic/historical: *historic* means "noteworthy, highly significant," whereas *historical* means "pertaining to history, relevant to the passage of time." Although the two terms are sometimes used interchangeably, they ought not to be. Since any event takes place in time—in that it figures implicitly in the onward movement of history—to speak of "an historical event" is really to speak redundantly. One might very well, however, find occasion to speak of "an historic event," meaning thereby an event that had a special significance, that was noteworthy for some special aspect or character.

homogeneous/homogenized: *homogeneous* means "of the same kind or nature, of a uniform structure"; *homogenized* refers to the fact that elements of a substance or population have been blended or processed into a uniform consistency. Therefore, something that has undergone homogenization can then be said to be (to have become, to have been made) homogeneous. Homogenized milk is milk in which the fat globules have been broken up, the resulting particles then caused to be distributed evenly throughout the liquid; one might say of the final mixture that in it the various elements of whole milk have been made homogeneous with one another. One might in this sense speak (somewhat figuratively) of the homogenization of a population, implying thereby that original differences—of race, nationality, religion—have been overcome or rendered less pronounced. Thus, a population might be considered homogeneous on the

basis of an original uniformity of characteristics or in consequence of a period of homogenization.

homophone/homonym: two words that have the same sound (are
pronounced the same) but have different spellings are homophones; two words that have the same sound (are pronounced
the same) but that have different meanings are homonyms. Consider words like *pear* and *pair* or *great* and *grate* or *seem* and
seam; these are homophones. Consider now a word like *bank*,
which can mean (among other things) "a place for business
transactions involving money and credit" and "the land adjoining a river"; or *air*, which can mean (among other things) "a
breeze or gust of wind" and "a melody." *Bank* and *air* are
homonyms. With homophones, we have two meanings converging on words that have the same pronunciation but different
spellings. With homonyms, we have two meanings converging
on words that exhibit the same spelling and pronunciation.
From the definitions, it should be clear that determining when
two words are homophones is relatively straightforward. The
question as it applies to homonyms, however, is not so easy to
answer, for with homonymy it is necessary to distinguish between the case where the two different meanings are meanings
of the same word and the case where they are meanings of different words. We have homonymy only when the latter condition is satisfied. The criterion for when the different meanings
are correlated with different words is that the words have different etymologies. The separate meanings given here for *bank* and
air trace back to different etymologies and thus may be counted
as meanings of different words. Consider now the word *mess*: It
can mean "a dirty or sloppy condition" or "a meal taken together" or "a group usually taking their meals together." All
these meanings go back to the same etymological source: Latin
miss(us), "something sent," through Old French, where it meant
"a course served at a meal," a meaning that came with the word
when it was borrowed into Middle English, from which time its
meaning has apparently burgeoned in our language. Or consider

the word *profile*, which can be used to mean either a side view of something or a biographical essay that touches only upon the high points in a subject's life or career. However, even though multiple meanings can be cited for these words, and even though the bearers of those meanings are pronounced identically, we are not dealing here with homonyms, since the different meanings derive from a single etymological source. The problem is caused by the fact that meanings tend to expand, to multiply, to proliferate. Words tend toward and ultimately achieve a state of polysemy. Most words, therefore, have not simply a meaning, but rather a range of meanings. Therefore, unless some discriminating criterion is introduced, homonymy would be found to exist throughout the lexicon. But, as mentioned earlier, there is such a criterion. For two words with the same pronunciation but with different meanings to constitute a case of homonymy, the trail must lead back to distinct etymologies. This is indeed the case with *bank* and *air* (consult any dictionary) but not with *mess* and *profile*.

hopeful/hopefully: *hopeful* is one of a class of adjectives that are predicated primarily of humans. Although we make use of expressions like "hopeful glance," "hopeful expression," and the like, these are derivative—one might almost say metaphoric—uses; primarily, it is people who we say are "hopeful," and it is thus people who do things "hopefully." Thus, it is when describing people that *hopefully* is used—a person *does* something hopefully; compare "John entered the contest hopefully," meaning that he entered the contest hoping he would win. As a variant of the preceding sentence, one might say, "Hopefully, John entered the contest." In constructions like the latter, even though *hopefully* modifies an entire clause, that clause describes an activity engaged in by a person, and the adverb performs its appropriate function of indicating the manner in which the subject carried out the activity. Consider now a pair of sentences like (1) "Hopefully, the show will be a success" and (2) "Hopefully, I will get the part." In (1), the requirement that the subject of the clause be a person is not satisfied (shows cannot be hopeful [nor envious, fearful, and so on]), so that *hopefully* is not being properly used, that is, to describe the manner in which an activity is being carried out. In sentence (2), however, the subject of the clause *is* a person and yet the use of *hopefully* is, strictly speaking, again contraindicated. Compare now with (2) the sentence (3) "Hopefully, I prepared for the coming interview"; now both sentences appear to comment on a human activity, and yet, although (3) passes muster, (2) is questionable. Grammatically, the difference seems to be that whereas in (3) *hopefully* modifies the verb, in (2) it modifies the entire clause, that is, it functions as a sentence adverb—in the manner of words like *indubitably, arguably, regrettably*, and so on. Sentence adverbs of this sort do not modify individual words but offer, instead, a general comment—a qualifying judgment by the speaker—on the situation described by the main clause of the sentence. On analogy with words of this type, it would turn out that the etymologically motivated form for the expression of what speakers intend in constructions like (2) is not *hopefully* but *hopeably*. The form *hopefully*, however, is too well entrenched in current usage to expect that this suggestion has any chance of being adopted; in fact, with the passing of a certain generation of speakers, the disapproval with which some superannuated specimens regard its use will have passed from the linguistic scene.

horrendous/horrible/horrific: the Latin word underlying these three forms is *horreo*, a verb whose infinitive meant "to stand on end" (in reference to hairs or bristles), a process that in animals and, to a lesser extent, in humans is a reaction to a fearsome or dreadful sight or spectacle. The slight meaning differences that may be gleaned from a comparison of the three words is thus a function of the different suffixes. The following meanings might be assigned to the three words: *horrendous*, "fearsome, frightful, dreadful"; *horrible*, "tending to arouse fear or dread"; *horrific*, "tending to cause fear or dread." These are rather finespun differences. In the following sentences, the words are used so that the slight meaning differences are required by or are adjusted to the event or incident that accompanies each word: (1) "Just ahead of us two cars collided in a horrendous accident," (2) "Last night I had a horrible nightmare," and (3) "The approach of the tornado was a horrific spectacle." As between *horrendous* and *horrible*, the difference might be put as follows: Something horrendous must be seen, something horrible need merely be experienced.

hypercorrection: a mistake in usage caused by the carrying over of a correction from a form or construction to which it properly applies to a form or construction to which it does not. Thus, when corrected for pronouncing present participial forms with a dropped final *g*, namely, as *runnin', talkin', holdin'*, and so forth, a person will "overcorrect" by pronouncing words like *happen, captain, kitchen*, with a final *g*. Another example: Corrected for using "John and me" in a sentence like "John and me grew up together" and told that the correct form in such constructions is "John and I," the speaker will then improperly extend the correction into sentences like "The teacher asked John and I to stay after school." The commission of hypercorrection is a sign of grammatical insecurity; it betrays an uncertainty about the proper application of grammatical rules. Not clear about the domain of the rule, the speaker applies it indiscriminately—to those forms and constructions where it does not apply as well as to those where it does.

if indeed: in most cases, *if* is all that is required. *If indeed* is relevantly used when a possibility has been mentioned, and in a subsequent sequence that possibility is again alluded to, as in the sequence "John said that he had returned my copy of *The Deerslayer; if indeed he did, I must have lost it.*"

illicit/illegal: both words mean "not permitted, not licensed," or "prohibited," but with *illicit* the prohibition will as a rule derive from a social convention, whereas with *illegal* it will be a function of a law or an otherwise constituted system of rules. In general, it will be a form of conduct that will be illicit and a type of practice that will be illegal. A love affair between a man and a woman, one of whom is married to someone else, would be illicit, whereas a marriage between such a man and woman would be illegal; the former relationship, in most cultures, transgresses a social or religious convention, the latter violates a civil law.

illumine/illuminate: both forms signify a production, or giving off, of light; in *illumine*, however, the emphasis is on the source from which the light is emanating, whereas in *illuminate* it is on the projection of the light onto a surface or into an area. Thus, an actress might be said to illumine a stage (an area that stagehands would illuminate) but to illuminate a text; it would be her presence that illumined the stage, her performance that illuminated the text. The word *luminous* is in closer semantic affinity with *illumine* than it is with *illuminate*. In saying a performance is luminous, we highlight the giving off of light, not the light given off, emphasizing the role of the performer, not the effect on the audience.

illusion/delusion: an illusion is an image or conception of something actual or real that presents itself to the mind in an abnormal or distorted manner; a delusion is a false belief about oneself or other people that persists despite its being at variance with the facts. Compare (1) "Gep Heym was under the illusion that he was the ace of the bullpen" and (2) "Gep Heym was under (suffered from) the delusion that he was the ace of the bullpen." A person may be disabused more readily of an illusion than of a delusion, so that consistent with these two sentences would be (3) "Heym's illusion that he was the ace of the bullpen was shattered when his earned run average was compared with those of Hagerty and Miller" and (4) "Heym's delusion that he was the ace of the bullpen persisted no matter what statistics were advanced." A delusion is a more pronounced departure from reality than is an illusion, frequently constituting, or being associated with, a psychotic condition.

impact/effect: the meaning of *impact* is that of the striking of one body against another, a collision; the focus of its meaning is on the point, the area, where the two bodies meet. The meaning of *effect*, by contrast, focuses on what happens as a consequence of the contact. Thus, whereas the impact made by one body on another might be to dent or crack the second body at the point of contact, the effect of one body striking another might be to cause the second body to recoil, swerve, or roll away. An impact is made, an effect is caused. To be sure, dealing with these meanings as they affect bodies is to deal with only a limited range of the relevant meanings. But the restriction brings into relief the point in question, which is that in recent usage the use of *impact* has been strikingly extended. In the process its meaning has been enervated to the point where it has become synonymous with that of *effect. Impact* is properly used in sentences like the following: "The car struck the wall with a terrific impact," "The impact of the bat against the ball made a clean, sweet sound." In sentences like the following, however, it simply represents an overdrawn usage: "I knew that this revelation would have a serious impact on her psyche," "I wondered what impact the revelation would have on her." The focus intended in such sentences is not on the proximate result produced by the revelation; the intended focus is, rather, on the consequences or sequelae of that revelation, a point that *effect* would effectively make. Notice that *have* correlates naturally with *effect* and *make* with *impact.*

The excess we are speaking of has impacted also on the use of *impact* as a verb (this sentence, in fact, instantiates the excess in question). Compare "Passage of this measure would impact disastrously on the consumer," "This development will impact earnings negatively," and "There is no question but that his resignation will impact the fortunes of the corporation for many months." In such sentences the use of *impact* suggests that the results of the "impacting" were immediate, occurred at the point of impact, as it were, when in fact the results are to be understood as anticipated, as taking "effect" in the course of time.

These sentences should be recast using *affect*. The following sentence, uttered by a politician, cries out for the replacement: "I hope this does not impact on the real progress of the budget and the tax legislation."

imply/infer: a speaker (or writer) implies, a hearer (or reader) infers; implications are incorporated in statements, inferences are deduced from statements. Compare "What you say (i.e., the statement you make) implies that you're unhappy with the arrangements," "I infer from what you say (i.e., from the statement you make) that you're unhappy with the arrangements." Further, "There's an implication (in what you say) that you're unhappy with the arrangements" and "I draw the inference (from what you say) that you're unhappy with the arrangements." A sentence of the sort, "Are you inferring that milk is not good for you?" is sometimes heard when *imply* would be the correct form to use. The only possible use for such a sentence would be when the speaker of that sentence infers from something that the interlocutor has said that the interlocutor has made that inference from something that the speaker has previously said. A witness before a Senate investigating committee expressed his dissatisfaction with the tenor of the questioning by saying: "I resent the inference of the senator." In the event, however, the senator had drawn no inference—merely having implied quite a few things.

import/importance: a sentence recently encountered: "As the preceding anecdote implies, beauty was of great import to Fanny." The author of this sentence has made a selectional detour around *importance*, the obvious word for this context, and presented instead the semantically disfiguring *import*. The motive here, as in similar cases where a phonetically similar but less usually used word is substituted is, by avoiding the obvious, to confer upon the writing a linguistic "cachet" (cf. the article on *intent/intention*). But the substitution of *import* for *importance* in the present context produces the difference between indicating that beauty was of great significance to Fanny and indicating that it was of great moment to her. Of course, this difference would perhaps not be disavowed by the author of the sentence; it might even be welcomed as an unexpected windfall. But this reaction (and the cavalier approach to language that it implies) conduces toward a general sloppiness in the use of language and ultimately to its cheapening.

impractical/impracticable: the fundamental semantic difference is represented in the two following definitions: *Impractical* means "not advisable to put into practice"; *impracticable* means "not capable of being put into practice." Thus, compare the contrasting meanings conveyed by (1) "an impractical scheme" and (2) "an impracticable scheme"; phrase (1) comments dubiously on the scheme's utility, (2) comments negatively on its feasibility.

in terms of: particularly in speech, this phrase seems to be on everyone's lips. Whenever a connection needs to be made between two grammatical units—of whatever sort—*in terms of* is invoked. It has become a veritable connective-of-all-trades. Here are a few examples recently heard: (1) "Casey was not clear in terms of his role in the office," (2) "I'll be talking to my board in terms of whether we should negotiate further," (3) "I can't answer in terms of what the judge decided," (4) "Her reaction is typical in terms of women who have been harassed," and (5) "Oil prices are going up probably in terms of the winter season." In (1) the phrase is substituting for *about* or *concerning*, in (2) it substitutes for *about*, in (3) it substitutes for *concerning*, in (4) it substitutes for *of*, and in (5) it substitutes for *because*. Each one of the items for which *in terms of* is substituted is a simple enough connective; however, each one is selected on the basis of some logical or grammatical connection between the units that are connected therewith; in other words, proper selection of a connective requires that the relation between the two connected units be understood. *In terms of* apparently neutralizes this requirement. Its virtue seems to be that in its use as a mere "counter," it is denatured of all logical or syntactic force and connects units paratactically—that is, simply juxtaposes them without indicating subordination, modification, or any other type of grammatical relation. The speaker is thus spared the necessity to think about the logical relation that subsists between the grammatical units being connected. In the following examples the phrase is properly used: (6) "The new models have more power, in terms of the number of channels they enable the user to reach"; (7) "Of the two candidates, Darr was the more effective speaker, in terms of his ability to appeal to the deep-seated longings of his listeners"; (8) "I have never heard a more alarming report, in terms of the threat that inheres in its third and fourth conditions." In these sentences the phrase "in terms of" picks up and refers to a noun in the preceding clause and expands upon the meaning of that noun; thus, in (6) the noun *power* is expanded upon, in (7) *speaker*, in (8) *report*.

incentive/inducement: both words have as a meaning component the sense of "something that motivates or persuades." There is, however, a subtle difference in the temporal orientation implied by the two words. Compare the following sentences: (1) "It was Nancy's wish to retire at an early age that provided the incentive for her to save a substantial part of her salary each week" and (2) "It was Nancy's conversation with her father that served as the inducement for her to save a substantial part of her salary each week." Exchange of our two words in these sentences would introduce in each a slight sense of semantic disorientation. The reasons appear to be something like the following: The motivation associated with an incentive is one in which the emphasis is on the consequences that will follow from implementation of the motivating factor—in (1), it is the prospect of retirement at an early age, but the motivation associated with an inducement, however, is one where the emphasis is on the factor that provided the motivation; in (2), it is Nancy's conversation with her father. In other words, the temporal orientation of *incentive* is toward the future, that of *inducement* is toward the past.

incident/incidence: the primary meaning of *incident* is that of an occurrence or event; the primary meaning of *incidence* is that of the rate or number of times at which something occurs. The following sentences illustrate these senses: "I witnessed an unusual incident the other day" and "The incidence of suicide among teenagers is increasing." Lately, however, one is encountering sentences in which *incidence* is used in the former sense, as in "A number of unusual incidences have occurred lately." Some dictionaries apparently sanction the use of *incidence* with this sense, but the usage has dubious credentials. It probably results from a confusion in which the plural of *incident* is aligned phonetically with the singular of *incidence*. In the face of this misalignment, a speaker unconsciously regards *incidents/incidence* as a singular and forms a new plural *incidences* by what we might call "front-formation," a process in which an original plural is regarded as a singular and a new plural is formed. (This process would then be the opposite of back-formation [which see].) The same confusion that besets *incident/incidence* is apparently at work in dislodging the words comprising the pair *precedent/precedence* from their inflectional moorings. One now hears uses like the following: "In deciding to advertise on television, the company has established a new precedence" and "There is no precedence for this claim." These singular uses imply the plural *precedences*, and it is fair to assume that lying behind this usage is the same confusion between plural and singular that we saw earlier in the case of *incident/incidence*, that is, because of phonetic similarity, *precedents* and *precedence* have merged in the linguistic consciousness of some speakers, with the result in this case not that usage tolerates a new plural (with *incidences* replacing *incidents*) but a new singular—*precedence* replacing *precedent*.

incredible/uncredible: a commentator recently said of a certain story that it was uncredible. By characterizing the story with the latter word rather than with the word *incredible*, he was drawing a definite distinction. Consider, for example, the phrases (1) "incredible story" and (2) "uncredible story": These are not synonymous. The commentator would use phrase (1) if he doubted the story, but he would use (2) if what he doubted was the story's teller. The one word questions truth, the other, veracity. Our commentator was, of course, unwilling to credit the story, but more than that, he was withholding belief from the narrator.

indecision/indecisiveness: compare (1) "After weeks of indecision, the president decided to take action on a tax bill" and (2) "After weeks of indecisiveness, the president decided to take action on a tax bill." The inference from (1) is that no one, neither the president, nor any of his advisers, was offering any determinative proposals concerning a tax bill and that the president finally decided to take matters into his own hands, whereas from (2) the inference is that the president was irresolute, that he could not decide what to recommend about taxes. *Indecision*, in other words, describes a general state or condition, one that can characterize a body or group, whereas *indecisiveness* describes an individual character trait. Therefore, *indecision* suggests merely the failure to arrive at a decision, without any implication of blame or responsibility, whereas *indecisiveness* implies a person's inability to reach a decision and amounts to a criticism of a person's character. Another difference between the two words lies in the fact that *indecisiveness* may refer to a series of decisions, each one superseding and canceling the previous one(s), with the result that no definite decision is reached; in this context, *indecision* simply means the absence of any decision, the putting into abeyance the making of a decision.

ineffectual/ineffective: *ineffectual* refers to a general or habitual lack of success in the carrying out of one's projects; *ineffective* refers to a specific or definite failure to perform a task or accomplish a purpose. One would characterize a person as ineffectual, his performance at a task or enterprise as ineffective. Comparing (1) "John's efforts were ineffective" and (2) "John's efforts were ineffectual," we infer from both sentences that John's efforts were unavailing; from sentence (2), however, we infer additionally that John applied himself, that he tried, and that his failure to accomplish his purpose was attributable to ineptitude; this inference does not necessarily follow from (1), which simply reports that John's efforts failed of their purpose. The semantic affinity of the word *feckless* consists more with *ineffectual* than it does with *ineffective*. One speaks more properly of a feckless person than of a feckless performance.

informer/informant: although these two words are listed in most dictionaries as synonyms, it is possible—and worthwhile—to draw a distinction between them. Both words refer to a person who informs, but *informant* has a specialized meaning in the field of linguistics, where it is used to refer to a native speaker of a language, someone who provides samples of that language that the linguist then proceeds to analyze. From this point of view, what an informant provides is not so much information as it is data, and we may use this fact to distinguish between *informant* and *informer*, using the latter term to describe someone who provides information, particularly if it is of a negative nature and serves some purpose of the one giving that information. Against this background, we should probably call someone an informant even if that person provided information, as long as the information provided was factual and objective, with no personal motive involved: An observer from whom testimony was being taken regarding what took place at the scene of an accident or in the commission of a crime might by this criterion be referred to as an informant. Consistent with this conclusion is the fact that the opprobrium that usually attaches to an informer in no way applies to an informant.

ingenious/ingenuous: the affinity projected by these two words is a function of spelling, not meaning. Semantically (as well as etymologically) the two words are quite dissimilar: *Ingenious* means "clever, resourceful, inventive," whereas *ingenuous* means "innocent or naive." Mention might as well be made here of the word *disingenuous*, which means "artful or unstraightforward." However, because of the word's formation—the "dis"-ing or recantation of *ingenuous*—its meaning is somewhat layered, conveying a sense not merely of unstraightforwardness but of false show, of craftiness, of a guileful design. A disingenuous reply is not simply a false or inappropriate reply; it is one calculated to mislead, to conceal the grounds that actually lie behind it.

instinctively/instinctually: the following sentence recently appeared in a local newspaper: "According to her lawyer, Mrs. X, in killing her son's molester, acted instinctually." Why was "instinctually" used and not the more common "instinctively?" In other words, was the lawyer, in making this observation, proceeding on the basis of some private semantic insight, or did this lawyer simply suppose that one of our two forms served the purpose as well as the other? There is good reason to believe that the choice was not arrived at indifferently, that it reflected, rather, a canny calculation. Although most dictionaries will list *instinctual* as a mere bye-form of *instinctive*, with no difference in meaning between the two, there are grounds for a distinction to be drawn according to which *instinctual* conveys the fundamental meaning "deriving from (based on) instinct" (rather than, say, reason, impulse, or reflection), whereas *instinctive* conveys the derivative meaning "immediate, involuntary, unthinking" (cf. "In reaching out to keep her son from falling, Dorothy reacted instinctively"). Given this semantic distinction, we may suppose that the lawyer is planning a defense based on the argument that the murder was an act that was inherently natural to a mother, one deriving from a primordial protective instinct, rather than to argue that it was an act of rashness committed on the spur of the moment. Readings with either form convey the meaning that the act of murder was spontaneous, but as instinctive, it is an act in which the normal control exercised by reason, conscience, and morality has been momentarily suspended, whereas as instinctual, it is rationalizable as a surrender to an irresistible urge, one committed in response to an overpowering maternal constraint, an act, in short, that anyone knowing the relationship that a mother bears to a son would understand, appreciate, and, ultimately, condone.

intense/intensive: in a letter to the editor of a newspaper, the following sentence appears: "Your article . . . fails to mention . . . the intensive pressure, sometimes cruelly unhealthy, on the contestants." Is *intensive* the right word here, or should the writer have used *intense*? As a meaning for *intense,* the dictionary gives "existing or occurring in a high or extreme degree"; for *intensive,* the meaning "characterized by intensity"; *intensity* in turn means "the quality or condition of being intense." These definitions wind around in a circle and do not offer grounds for deciding which of the two forms is more appropriate in the cited context. At the same time, a semantic scruple constrains us against concluding that since both words refer to the notion of intensity, the two forms are simply synonyms and that it makes no difference which of the two we use; no, we need to take it seriously when our linguistic intuition balks at a particular usage. Consider again the context of "pressure." It seems that we properly adjudicate the issue if we say that when the intensity is exerted at the source of the pressure, then the correct form is *intense,* whereas if the intensity is exerted at the point of application, then *intensive* is the form that is motivated. Thus, in "The committee exerted intense pressure on the contestants to comply" and "Gases subjected to high temperatures produce intensive pressure on the walls of their containers," the two words are properly employed.

intent/intention: following is a sentence that appeared recently in a local newspaper: (1) "I have never had any intent of cohabiting with him." What is there about the sense of *intent* that raises a question about its use in this sentence? Someone who is intent on a certain purpose has a fixed, steady determination to realize that purpose. The noun *intent* carries over this sense of steady determination. An intention, however, is simply a commitment to do something at some future time or other. Sentence (1) expresses the idea that at no time was the subject's mind preoccupied with the determination to cohabit with a certain man, whereas what is intended is that at no time did she form the resolution to cohabit with him. *Intent* implies a sustained, unbroken commitment not to cohabit, but *intention* would imply an intermittent resolution not to do so. As sentence (1) is formulated, it would be possible for the subject to deny having the intent to cohabit and still have or have had the intention to cohabit.

interval/interlude: intervals occur in a variety of modes. In its most usual meaning, however, an interval is a gap in time (or space), whereas an interlude generally functions to fill such a gap, thus, to occupy an interval. In music, both the space between the notes and the time required to traverse this space constitute intervals, and although, for theoretical reasons, it is not possible for interludes to fill intervals of this type, there are various musical contexts in which interludes do figure. Thus, a type of composition inserted into a work of a different nature can function as an interlude; a passage scored for instruments would be an interlude in an oratorio, for example, as would a vocal passage in the movement of a symphony. Moreover, in a stage play a musical piece might serve as an interlude (an entr'acte) filling the interval between successive acts.

intrinsic/innate: both words mean "belonging to the essential nature of (a thing)," but *innate* adds to this meaning the component "by virtue of being born in, or being native to." Boastfulness may be intrinsic to a certain man's character, but one would not claim that he had been born with that trait, whereas intelligence, as a purely mental function, is not only intrinsic to a human being's organic constitution, but it is also innate to it.

involve/entail: both words describe some sort of relation or connection between entities, but that relation is of a particular nature when *entail* is used, in that if *b* is entailed by *a* then *b* *necessarily* accompanies or follows from *a*. Compare "Expanding the police force would entail raising taxes," that is, the raising of taxes would be a certain, an unavoidable, consequence of expanding the police force. The use of *involve* in a sentence like this would not so definitively indicate that a strictly causal relationship obtained between the two acts. But in a sentence like "A successful sales campaign usually entails the distribution of samples," where *involve* might appropriately be used, *entail* would represent an inflated usage. And similarly, in the following: "Nothing has proven more effective this political year than trumpeting a plan to save the economy. And nothing has proven more dangerous than laying out what such a plan would entail." The intention here is to focus on what the plan would contain, what it would include, not on what it would lead to, what consequences it would have. The word that should have been used is *involve*. It might be mentioned that the phrase *necessarily entails* contains a redundancy, and the phrase *usually entails* hints at a misuse.

irate/irascible: consider the sentence (1), which was recently overheard: "Henry became very irascible." No doubt, what was intended was (2) "Henry became very irate." *Irate* means "angry"; *irascible* means "disposed toward or easily provoked to anger." Sentence (1) might have a use in a situation where Henry, who was previously of a calm and easygoing nature, began suddenly to show what for him were uncharacteristic signs of being easily and suddenly provoked to anger. If, however, a person's anger were to be motivated by something in the immediate context, that person should be said to have become irate, not irascible. Like (1) would be (3) "Henry became very moody (or "complacent")." Like *irascible*, the predicates in (3) refer to personality traits and, as such, changes in them would likely reflect developments over time, not result from contingent changes in the circumstantial surroundings.

Notice that we say "He's an irascible type of person," not "He's an irate type of person."

irregardless: an arrant solecism; *regardless* means "without regard," so that *irregardless* means "not without regard," hence "with regard," so that a speaker in uttering a sentence like "Irregardless of my parents' wishes, I am going to marry my cousin," is probably expressing exactly the opposite of the meaning intended. At work here is probably some unwitting contamination by the form *irrespective*; but, of course, since there is in this case no *-less* suffix, the prefix properly performs its normal function, that of negating the meaning of the base to which it is attached.

. . . is is . . . : when occurring in an expression like "What this is is a direct violation of our regulations," the first *is* stands in for a phrase like *amounts to*, and the resulting construction, although awkward, is not ungrammatical. The same sequence, however, is sometimes heard in an expression like "If you put them on that way, what happens is is that the shingles fall off the roof," with a slight pause after the first *is*. In this usage, that *is* is not standing in for anything, is completely redundant, and the resulting construction is a solecism. The same applies to an environment in which this redundancy occurs even more frequently, when used in "The fact is is . . ." Thus, we hear people saying things like "The fact is is that people want more services." What is the fact? Simply—that people want more services.

The following is another form that the error takes: "The problem is is that . . . "

it's: the typographical form for the contraction of "it is"—to be sharply distinguished from the possessive form of the neuter pronoun *it*, the proper form of which is *its*, that is, without the apostrophe. The following sentences show these two words in their proper typographic forms: (1) "It's a story about the difficult life of orphans" and (2) "Its home is in the woods." Compare to the second sentence the sentences "His home is in the woods" and "Her home is in the woods." The comparison brings into focus the possessive function of the form *its* in (2).

Janus words: words are so called when they mean two opposing things, when they, as it were, look in opposite semantic directions at the same time. Among the words that have this two-faced semantic property are *let*, which may mean both "to allow" and "to hinder," and *fast*, meaning both "quick" and "immovable." A more interesting type of such word is found among certain adjectives that describe human characteristics; thus, a word like *suspicious*, when applied to a person, as in "Henry is a suspicious person," may be interpreted to mean either that Henry suspects people or that people suspect Henry. The same property is evinced by a word like *curious*. A person so described may be curious about things or be deemed an object of curiosity. Consider also the adjective *moot*, which may mean either "capable of being argued" or "having no practical significance"; or, to cast the meanings in a form that more closely expresses the contradictory aspects of its meaning: "substantive" and "vacuous." An interesting case is represented by the word *betray* in a use like the following: "In speaking those words, Tom betrayed himself." Does this mean that Tom unwittingly disclosed something to others, or does it mean that he violated a deeply held principle of his own?

join/conjoin: things may be joined by nature, that is, in their physical constitution, but if they are conjoined, they have been made so. Thus, to be joined is to be in a certain state; to conjoin is to perform an act or make a decision. A person's hand is joined to the wrist, but a prosthetic hand might be conjoined with the wrist. In the same way, the lower forty-eight states are joined with one another to form the lower United States, but Hawaii and Alaska are conjoined with these to form the greater United States. (The sense of *join* in a use like that in "Dudley joined the Wynnefield Boosters" lies outside these considerations.)

jovial/jocular: *jovial* refers to a mood or disposition, *jocular* to a conduct or manner. A jovial person is characterized by heartiness and good spirits, a jocular person by a propensity for joking.

joyful/joyous: although one may say either (1) "The wedding was a joyous occasion" or (2) "The wedding was a joyful occasion," slightly different implications are signaled by the respective versions. In (1) the implication is that the wedding, *as an affair*, was an occasion for joy, whereas in (2) the implication is that those attending the wedding, *the participants*, experienced a feeling of joy. Although the distinction is not generally observed, strict usage would assign joyfulness to people, joyousness to occasions; moreover, although *joyful* appears to have successfully extended its range of application—to inanimate affairs like weddings and other types of joy-inducing occasions—*joyous* has apparently been less successful in its efforts at range extension: There is still something semantically challenging about an expression like "Stu Bobb was a joyous person." The sense that projects itself from this sentence is that Stu Bobb was a person who *afforded* joy.

judicial/judicious: *judicial* refers to judgment as it is exercised by the court, *judicious* to judgment as exercised by an individual. Therefore, we have "That's a judicial matter," meaning one for the courts to consider, and "He's a judicious person," meaning a person who is careful in the making of judgments. Exchange of these two forms in these contexts would not be well tolerated: "That's a judicious matter" would simply be wrong, whereas "He's a judicial person," although not as outlandish, would have to be interpreted as describing someone connected with the judicial form of government, a thought that would be better expressed by "He belongs to the judiciary" or, simply, by "He's a judge."

A recent newspaper column concerning the activity of the Supreme Court was captioned "judicious activism." This suggested an activism on the part of the Court that was characterized by prudence and good judgment, a conclusion that the notion of an activist court had not in the past supported. Sure enough, in reading the article it became clear—what with its references to "judicial conservatism," "judicial restraint," and "judicial style"—that the caption was inappropriate, that it should have read "judicial activism." In other words, the article dealt with an activism displayed by the Court (in fact, by one of the justices), hence, a judiciary activism.

kudos: this word, meaning "acclaim or praise," is a (transliterated) borrowing from Greek; in line with the declension to which it belongs in Greek, its plural form would have been *kudea*. But it seems to have been used only as a singular in Greek, and the English form is itself singular. However, one finds it frequently misconstrued as a plural, and the form *kudo* used when a single bit of praise is intended, as in "I would like to offer a kudo to the president for his stand on the pending legislation." In a usage of this kind, there are really two errors: Like the words *acclaim* or *praise*, *kudos* is an abstract noun; as such, it does not normally permit of quantification or apportionment. Thus, in addition to the inappropriate form *kudo*, the use of the indefinite article in the sentence is also mistaken. The proper form of the sentence would be "I would like to offer kudos to the president for his stand on the pending legislation." (Despite the preceding considerations, however, someone having used the form *kudo* may rationalize its use as an instance of back-formation [which see]).

lay/laid: consider the following sentence, recently encountered in a popular magazine: "Visitors today can see a small, decorative arch where, it is said, a craftsman immediately lay down his tools to go enlist when he heard the news of the Japanese attack on Pearl Harbor." One can say that a person lay down, that is, assumed a reclining position, but not that someone lay something down. In that use, when the verb takes an object, the proper form is *laid*. The portion of the sentence earlier referred to should therefore have read ". . . a craftsman immediately laid down his tools . . . " *Lie* is an intransitive verb, whose principal parts are *lie, lay, lain*. The other verb is *lay*, a transitive verb, whose principal parts are *lay, laid, laid*. The problem arises with the respective past tenses of the two verbs. Part of the difficulty in keeping these two forms straight lies in the fact that both verbs pattern with the adverb *down* (phonetically, there is no appreciable difference between *lay down* and *laid down)*, but the key factor in determining which form to use is whether a direct object follows the verb or not: If it does, the proper form is *laid*; otherwise, *lay*.

less/fewer: among the nouns of English, two of the major classes are those referred to as "mass" nouns and those referred to as "count" nouns. Nouns like *sugar, toast, coffee*, and *rice* are mass nouns, and those such as *pencil, stone, tree*, and *biscuit* are count nouns. Mass nouns refer to things that occur as collected or undifferentiated compositions—that occur in the mass; count nouns refer to individual units that, as such, can be counted. When one wishes to qualify members of these two classes as to a reduced quantity or amount, the correlation (a strict one) pairs *less* with mass nouns and *fewer* with count nouns. Thus, the following sentences reflect proper usage: "I'd like less sugar, please," "I'd like fewer biscuits, please." One can also say "I'd like fewer *grains* of rice" or ". . . fewer *cups* of coffee," *grain* and *cup* being count nouns. It is a mistake, however, to say things like the following: "I'd like less biscuits, please" and "There are less boys in my class than in yours." It is interesting that nouns of *both* classes are modified to a higher quantity with the form *more*: thus, "I'd like more sugar" and "I'd like more biscuits." Notice here, however, that the count noun is rendered as a plural. Compare in this connection "I'd like to see more sugars," where what is in question are *varieties* of sugar, that is, a countable number of different types of sugar.

It might be added that abstract nouns—those that refer to some notion or concept—pattern in this respect like the mass nouns: Just as one says "less rice" and "less coffee," so one says "less patience" and "less endurance."

lexicon/vocabulary/glossary/dictionary: a lexicon is the stock of words in a language. This word stock may exist, but it need not be assembled and listed in a book; essentially, it exists in an abstract sense as the body of words theoretically available to the speakers (users) of the language. A vocabulary is the stock of words controlled by a speaker of a language (one might speak of Shakespeare's vocabulary, for example, or the vocabulary of Thomas Jefferson). The rationale for drawing a distinction between a lexicon and a vocabulary is that it is one thing for a word to exist and be available, but it is another for speakers to be able to avail themselves of it; in other words, all the words in a language are in its lexicon, but speakers' vocabularies only contain those words whose meaning they know. Thus, *subfuscous* is in the lexicon of English, but until this moment it was not in my vocabulary. A glossary is the stock of words in a particular text (one may compile a glossary of a magazine issue, of Thackeray's *Vanity Fair,* or of a cookbook); a dictionary is a book listing the words of a language (its lexicon) along with their definitions, pronunciations, etymologies, and other such information. The vocabularies of individual speakers represent portions of a language's lexicon.

liable/likely: both words indicate a susceptibility to something or other, but whereas that susceptibility is essentially neutral (and may even be positive) where *likely* is concerned, it assumes a somewhat negative or unsatisfactory implication with the word *liable.* Compare the following sentences: (1) "Roger is liable to flunk his entrance exam" and (2) "Roger is likely to pass his entrance exam." We would say (3) "This paint is liable to peel in less than a year" and (4) "This paint is likely to last for a long time." If someone were to say either (5) "This paint is liable to last for a long time" or (6) "This paint is likely to peel in a short time," the inference would be that, despite what one would normally expect of this particular brand of paint, the speaker is venturing a guess that its performance may contravene expectations.

limits/limitations: in a recent publication, a reviewer remarked that President Truman's unpopularity derived, in part, from "his own limits as a politician." Why does this formulation grate against one's linguistic intuition? From the standpoint of an individual, limits are boundaries imposed by extrinsic factors, whereas boundaries or restrictions imposed by intrinsic factors are more properly understood as limitations. The proper word in this context would therefore be *limitations*, not *limits*. Among Truman's limits as a politician might be cited the Constitution of the United States or a Republican Congress, that is, such factors as limited the *scope* of his political efforts. His political limitations, however, might be his unwillingness to take advice or his reluctance to compromise. These, then, would be factors that would limit the *efficacy* of his political endeavors. This distinction between outer and inner constraints explains why we feel a sense of directional clash from the combination "own limits."

A related point: These days, as the problems associated with extended service in the Congress come more and more under voters' scrutiny and as measures begin to be proposed for dealing with those problems, the phrases "term limitations" and "term limits" occur with increasing frequency. Are both forms correct? Or is one of them to be preferred? To rephrase what was just said, a limit is a bound or boundary, a point beyond which one may not go, which may not be exceeded; a limitation, by contrast, is something that imposes such a bound or boundary. We speak of speed limits, city limits, the limits of a person's patience, and so on. But where limitations are concerned, we speak of the limitations on a person's freedom, on a judge's power, on a landlord's rights, and so on. These limitations follow from, are consequences of, stipulations contained in various kinds of legal documents. If a period of, say, twelve years should be imposed as the total length of time that a member of Congress should be allowed to serve, that period would thus count as a limit to the term; the legislation that enacted this law would then embody or constitute a limitation—not on the term but on the ability of members of Congress to serve longer than that term. Say *term limits*.

loath/loathe: *loath* is an adjective meaning "unwilling, reluctant, disinclined," whereas *loathe* is a verb meaning "to dislike intensely, to feel revulsion toward." Despite the similarity in their forms, they do not permit exchange in their respective functions. To be avoided, therefore, is a use like that in "Denny Hower was loathe to resign from the fraternity," where the verb is used instead of the adjective. Moreover, since the two words are pronounced differently, it is possible to make the counterpart of this mistake in speech. The adjective ends with the sound at the end of *bath*, whereas the verb ends with the sound at the end of *bathe*.

location/locality/locale: in general terms, we might say that a location is a place, a locality is an area within a place, and a locale is a place regarded as an environment. Compare (1) "Venice is situated in a most interesting location," (2) "Within Venice one runs into many an interesting locality," and (3) "Venice provides an interesting locale in which to hold movie festivals." In these sentences, *location* is used in (1), since the judgment of interest is made relative to the physical or geographical placement of a site; *locality* is used in (2), since there the judgment of interest relates to the individual character of specific places; and *locale* is used in (3), since there the judgment of interest relates to the events and activities that take place at a certain location. Against this background, the meanings of sentences (4) "What is to be the location of the summer revels this spring?" and (5) "What is the locale of your summer home?" should register as somewhat disoriented.

masterful/masterly: discussions of this pair usually attempt to validate a difference in usage on the basis that the two words have different meanings; thus, given for *masterful* are the meanings "imperious, domineering" and for *masterly* the meanings "expert, skilled." This makes it appear that both adjectives describe personal characteristics and that selection of one or the other form is determined by which sort of characteristic one wishes to refer to. However, the difference in the meanings has at its base a difference in predicability, that is, a difference in *the sort of thing* that the words may properly be applied to. We say "He was a masterful chairman," but "It was a masterly performance." The word *masterful*, in other words, is applied to the type of person that one is, *masterly* to the sort of thing that one does; *masterful* describes a person, *masterly* describes a performance. According to this distinction, the word *masterful* is misapplied in a sentence like the following: (1) "John did a masterful job of repairing my carburetor," although it could be used in a sentence like (2) "John was masterful in directing the meeting." Sentence (1) requires *masterly*.

maturation/maturity: in both words there is a meaning component signifying growth or development; in the meaning of *maturation*, however, this signification is directed more at the process of development; in that of *maturity* it is directed more at the attained state. When we speak, say, of a man's maturation as a scholar, the implicit focus is on the years that it took him to achieve that status, whereas when we speak of a man's maturity as a scholar, the focus is on his scholarship having reached fruition. A person experiences (lives through the process of) maturation but achieves (attains to the state of) maturity. There is a rough-and-ready fundamental dichotomy according to which maturation is a process undergone by plants and fruits, maturity a state arrived at by humans; thus, a plant maturates, a person matures. As suggested by the examples given herein, however, this dichotomy is not hard and fast.

may/might: as modal auxiliaries, these two forms have a variety of important functions, only one of which will figure in this article. These forms, in their so-called epistemic function, indicate degrees of possibility. Compare (1) "Fred may come to the party" (disregard the sense of "permission") and (2) "Fred might come to the party." In (1), the sense conveyed is that the situational background is neutral with respect to its containing anything that would impinge upon or compromise the possibility of Fred's coming to the party, whereas (2) conveys the sense that there exists in the background a certain contingency, one whose realization would cancel or minimize that possibility; he will come, say, if his sister does not arrive from upstate, if his cold has responded to treatment, and so forth. Compare now (3) "The Yankees may win the pennant next year" and (4) "The Yankees might win the pennant next year." Sentence (3) says essentially that the possibility that the Yankees will win the pennant next year is not to be ruled out, (4) raises the winning of the pennant as a possibility but implies that realization of this possibility depends on the actualization of certain unlikely developments—say, if the Yankees got lucky, if all their players had standout years, if the other teams collapsed, if fate decreed a change in their general partner, and so on. Sentence (3) just says it is possible; (4) says it depends (on the actualization of exceptional circumstances). In making the realization dependent on the occurrence or nonoccurrence of (these special) circumstances, the sense of possibility conveyed by *might* is seen to be weaker than that conveyed by *may*, which does not so constrain the range of possibilities.

The different grades of possibility conveyed by *may* and *might* play a significant role in certain common constructions, and more and more frequently, one encounters in such constructions an occurrence of *may* when *might* is clearly called for. Consider (5) "The doctor failed to use the procedure that may have prolonged the patient's life," (6) "The engineer ignored the signal that may have prevented the crash," and (7) "Too late he introduced measures that may have saved the bank from failing." In these sentences the impression is conveyed that *possibly*: (5) the life was prolonged, (6) the crash was prevented, (7) the bank was saved from failing. But since the sense in all these sentences is that the cited consequences in fact did not materialize (i.e., the life was *not* prolonged, and so on) *may* is contraindicated, and *might*, with its indication of weaker (in this case, nil) possibility is the proper form to use.

Another construction in which this error commonly occurs is one in which one of the clauses describes a condition that is "contrary to fact." Consider (8) "If Bush had not raised taxes, he may have won the presidency," (9) "My friend may have completed his novel, if he had not drunk so heavily," and (10) "If there had been more rain that summer, the flowers may have fared better." Here again, the use of *may* makes it appear that the events described in the main clauses of these sentences took place, when the fact is that they did not. In sentences of this type, the dependent clause makes reference to a contingency that has actually occurred and whose occurrence cancels the possibility alluded to in the main clause; thus, the fact that Bush raised taxes had the effect of reducing his chances to be president, and so *might*, with its sense of weakened possibility, is the appropriate form. The same analysis applies to (9) and (10). There is an intellectually jarring impression conveyed by the use of *may* in all such sentences, in that its use leaves possibility open, when we understand from the dependent clauses that events have in fact foreclosed it.

me/myself: *me* is the form taken by the accusative case of the first person singular personal pronoun; *myself* has two fundamental functions: as a reflexive pronoun, for example, in "I cut myself," and as an intensive, as used in "I myself had broken the vase." Consider now sentences like the following: "Our neighbors invited my wife and myself to a party," "The invitation was for John and myself," "This is a story about my brother and myself." In each of these sentences, good usage requires that the form following *and* should be the personal pronoun *me*, not the form *myself*. In a sentence like "The tickets were for him and myself," *him* indicates clearly that the word appearing in agreement with it should be in the accusative case, specifically, *me* (one would certainly not effect agreement by saying "The tickets were for himself and myself"). The use of *myself* in sentences like this simply betrays an uncertainty about proper usage, an unwillingness to commit oneself as between *I* and *me*. A related error is frequently encountered when the form *I* is in fact required and *myself* is used instead: Compare "My wife and myself went to the movies last night" and "Harry and myself were the instigators of the scheme." This is really a craven usage, and steps should be taken to eliminate it from one's practice.

metalanguage: one of the interesting things about language is that it is reflexive: It can discuss itself. In order to do this, however, it must suffer a modification. If it does not do so, it can (as it were) confound itself. Thus, there is something amiss about expressions like "Chicago contains three syllables," "Ice begins with an *i*," "He said to me if I can." The improprieties in these expressions can be amended by a modification of typography, thus: "'Chicago' contains three syllables," "'Ice' begins with an *i*," "He said to me, 'If I can.'" What the quotation marks in these expressions indicate is that it is the language itself that is being spoken of, meaning that under discussion are the words: *Chicago, ice,* and *if I can.* Language that is used to discuss or comment upon subject matter that is itself linguistic is referred to as metalanguage, that is, a language situated at a level above (Greek *meta-* "beyond") the level at which the language normally functions. Quotation marks placed around words indicate that it is the words themselves that are being discussed and not the entities that the words normally refer to. Thus, without quotation marks, *Chicago* refers to a city in Illinois, but "*Chicago*" refers to a word, namely, the word within the quotation marks. It is therefore correct to write both "Chicago is a great city" and "'Chicago' is trisyllabic." A corollary to the distinction between language and metalanguage is that between the use of a word and its mention. We say that *Chicago* is used in the sentence "Chicago is a great city," but that it is mentioned in "'Chicago' is trisyllabic." Notice that in both cases it is the word that is being referred to, not the referent of the word, that is, it is *Chicago* that is used or mentioned, not the city of that name.

metanalysis (or wrong division): it sometimes happens that the morphological boundaries between certain commonly juxtaposed words are improperly registered in the linguistic consciousness of certain speakers and that after a while the result of such metanalysis causes the remodeling of a word. It is in the nature of most such cases that the improper registration of these boundaries is masked by the particular character of the juxtapositions—that is, that a speaker's misapprehension regarding word boundaries will not betray itself in normal use of the language. Consider a word like *another* or a phrase like *an apple*. It would only be on the production of utterances like "The nother thing I don't like about David is . . ." or "I ate two napples yesterday" that we would infer that the speaker had all along, in saying things like "another thing" and "I ate an apple yesterday"—been analyzing these locutions incorrectly. If a man from Manhattan should say "I'm going out to the Guyland this weekend," we could infer that his understanding of the morphological structure of *Long Island* was deficient. The examples cited here have, as it happens, had no effect on the form of the words involved. But comparable cases in the development of the language have left consequences in the makeup of certain words. An interesting example is the word *nickname*. This form derives from the phrase "an ēke name," from a time when *eke* (our verb) could function also as an adjective, meaning "additional" or "extra." Other examples are *adder* from "a naddre," *newt* from "an ewte," *apron* from "a napron"; compare also the name *Ned* from "mīn Ed" (*mīn* being the form taken at an earlier stage of English by the possessive *my* when occurring before words beginning with a vowel).

method/methodology: a method is a way of doing things; a methodology is a body, a system, of methods. One can say "The methodology of the social sciences includes a number of techniques and procedures, one of which is statistical analysis," but one should not use the comprehensive word when what is in question is a particular technique or procedure. It is simply inflated usage to say "I did not approve of the methodology he used in preparing the walls for lacquering."

metonymy: a figure of speech in which something is referred to not as such but on the basis of a feature or characteristic that is culturally associated with it. On hearing that wedding bells will shortly be ringing for Marilyn, one understands that Marilyn is soon to be married. This knowledge is communicated in that there is a general association (both practically and in the general consciousness) between wedding bells and the marriage ceremony. Inasmuch, therefore, as there obtains this relation between wedding bells and marriage, *wedding bells* can be used to refer to marriage. Some common metonymies are *the White House* for the presidency, *the Vatican* for the pope, *the throne* for the king or queen, and the like.

miscegenation: this word is frequently analyzed (implicitly) as being composed of the prefix *mis-* and the remainder *-cegenation;* one infers this faulty analysis from the mispronunciation, frequently heard, in which the primary stress is placed on the first syllable, as though the meaning of *-cegenation* is being somehow negated or critiqued. The word has a different composition, however; its first element is not *mis-*, but *misce-*, from the Latin *miscere*, meaning "to mix" (cf. *miscible*); the remainder of the word contains then the root *genus*, the combination of elements yielding the meaning "to mix races or genera." To evince this (proper) analysis, the pronunciation should place primary stress on the syllable *-na-*, thus *miscegenátion*.

misinformation/disinformation: misinformation is information that is false; disinformation is information that is misleading or deceptive. Misinformation, though false, may be sincerely expressed: A man who expressed his firmly held conviction that smoking was not injurious to people's health would be purveying misinformation; it would, however, be disinformation if in an ad for cigarettes it were stated that the tar content had been reduced or that an improved type of paper was being used. These claims, though true, simply divert attention from the central question at issue where cigarettes are concerned—namely, their effect on smokers' health. Disinformation may contain some truth, but it will fail to mention additional facts that are essential to a thorough and unbiased understanding of the situation. Thus, a report from a pharmaceutical company describing the success of a medicine for a certain disease will cite extremely positive results but omit to mention that the patients selected for the treatment shared a certain favoring characteristic—of age, diet, or physical condition—the factoring in of which would necessitate reevaluation of the results. In the same way, it would be simply confusing the issue—and would thus constitute disinformation—if a cigarette advertisement were to point out that more people die in automobile accidents than from smoking cigarettes. As may be inferred from the preceding remarks, motive plays a crucial role in distinguishing between mis- and disinformation.

mistrust/distrust: the meanings differ in the sense that mistrust involves a withholding of confidence, whereas distrust involves a projection of lack of confidence or suspicion. Moreover, the suspicion attendant upon distrust is generally projected onto a person; the withholding of confidence characteristic of mistrust is usually occasioned by a feature in the background of a person's behavior or conduct. In a situation in which Emily's broker has submitted a plan for a stock swap, her husband, by way of attempting to dissuade his wife from participating, might say either "I distrust your broker" or "I mistrust your broker's motives." A sentence like "I don't trust Volney" means that I distrust Volney, not that I mistrust him. If I in fact distrust him, however, it would follow that I would withhold trust from any of his suggestions or proposals; in other words, on all such occasions I would mistrust his reasons or motives.

mitigate/extenuate: this article is concerned with the difference between the phrases "mitigating circumstances" and "extenuating circumstances." To mitigate is to lessen, moderate, make less severe; to extenuate is to stretch out, thin, make less dense or compact. Compare now (1) "Joey Donovan's behavior was certainly reprehensible, but there were extenuating circumstances." Would any difference be effected on (1) by substituting *mitigating* for *extenuating*? It would appear that extenuating circumstances have a bearing on Donovan's behavior, rendering what he did less weighty, less substantial, and for this reason not as reprehensible; mitigating circumstances, however, appear to bear on the degree of reprehensibility that should be attributed to Donovan, lessening the severity of that reprehensibility and making Donovan thereby less subject to blame for his behavior. The basis for this distinction seems to lie in the fact that extenuation applies to actions, whereas mitigation applies to consequences. It would be appropriate to say both "Rupert tried to extenuate Mary's conduct" and "Rupert tried to mitigate the effect of Mary's conduct," but exchange of the two verbs in these sentences would not likely be permitted.

mitigate/militate: *mitigate* means to reduce or lessen; *militate* means to have weight or effect and requires construction with a preposition (usually *against*). One might say "His poor manners mitigated his chances for success," but it is a mistake (one commonly made) to say "His poor manners mitigated against his chances for success." Replacing *mitigated* with *militated* in the latter sentence would make it acceptable usage—as would replacement in the following passage, which appeared in a letter to a major newspaper: "There are four basic ingredients necessary for any school to survive. The first is a competent principal. The political process now mitigates against this."

mix/mixture: both words refer to a combining of elements. The difference is that in a mixture, the combined elements lose their individual identities and are fused, blended, or compounded in the result, whereas in a mix, the elements, though combined, retain their individual identities. Thus, a martini is a mixture of gin and vermouth, a vinaigrette is a mixture of olive oil and vinegar; but an antipasto is a mix of salami, cheese, olives, greens, anchovies, and other ingredients. Similarly, a neighborhood might be a mix of races, nationalities, and income groups. By this criterion the result of combining motor oil and water is a mix. When the United States of America is conceived of as a melting pot, the implication is that the various races and ethnic groups making up its population will be rendered into a mixture; what in fact is produced, however, is more likely a mix. When the combination in question is of abstract elements, we are sometimes offered a choice: Compare "Lefty Blackman's attitude was a curious (1) mix (2) mixture of arrogance and solicitude." Version (1) suggests that arrogance and solicitude alternated in Blackman's attitude; (2) implies a judgment on the part of the observer that his attitude was a curious amalgam of the two characteristics.

momentarily/presently: a program host, taking a break for a commercial, said to his several guests, "I'll see you all again momentarily." *Momentarily* means "in a moment," and given the length of the customary commercial break, that word was inappropriate. A better choice would have been *presently*, which means simply "soon," or "shortly," without the implication that what is to take place will take place without the intervention of a time interval, or immediately. Consider the difference between (1) "The water will boil presently" and (2) "The water will boil momentarily." We could replace (1) with (3) "The water will be boiling presently," but (2) would produce an ungainly result if rendered as (4) "The water will be boiling momentarily." The reason for this difference in our responses is that, whereas *presently* allows for the duration of time between the time of utterance and the result, *momentarily* precludes any such interval and, for this reason, disallows, or clangs awkwardly with, use of the (future) progressive aspect.

moot point: the phrase is ambiguous in a curious, self-defeating sort of way: On the one hand, it means (1) a point that is worth taking up for discussion; on the other, it means (2) a point that it would be pointless—a waste of time—even to consider. Importantly, however, what renders the point pointless is not that no significance attaches to the question at issue; what renders it pointless, or moot, is that events or conditions are such that no significance would attach to whatever judgment or decision was arrived at. Thus, if Roger and Alice are engaged to be married, it might be a moot point in sense (1) to discuss whether or not they are suited to each other; the point or question would become moot in sense (2), however, if Alice or Roger broke off the engagement. Another example: Congressman X has served three terms in the House of Representatives. His qualifications to serve a fourth term may be mooted, that is, the question of whether he is qualified can become a moot point in sense (1). Should Congressman X decide not to run for a fourth term, however, the question of whether he is qualified to serve becomes a moot point in sense (2), namely, any decision would be empty, devoid of practical significance. As suggested herein, one can also moot a point, in other words, present it for purposes of discussion; this (verbal) sense correlates with the former of the two adjectival senses given here.

more important/importantly: the question where this usage is concerned involves sentences like (1) "In acquiring the services of Reds Ramsey, the Terriers obtained a .300 hitter, but more important, they plugged a defensive hole at second base." The case made for *more important* in a use like this is that it abbreviates the phrase "what is more important." Proponents of the form *more importantly* argue that if a substitute word should be used in this context, it would occur not in adjectival but in adverbial form, that is, it would occur as "more specifically," "more fundamentally," "more pertinently," and so forth. But this argument is not to the point. An adverbial phrase like *more specifically*, we should notice, is comparative. As such, it modifies a verb in two clauses; for example, consider the sentence "Baylis argued against passage of the law, but he argued more pointedly against the corporation's motive in proposing it." In this sentence the adverb *pointedly* applies to *argued* in both clauses. However, in sentence (1)—a sentence that is paradigmatic of the construction in question—an adverbial (*importantly*) could in no way be construed as comparatively modifying the verb in the two clauses, since the verb is different in each of the clauses. And this is the typical situation when *more important* is used. The reason that the form *more important* has developed in this context is probably that the phrase "what is more important" was originally felt to have a rhetorical value that such a phrase with other adjectives never suggested, and thus it is that shortening left us with *more important* but no other, comparable phrase.

motive/motivation: a motive is a reason for doing something, for acting in a certain way; a motivation is the result of having been supplied with a motive, and is thus a drive, a stimulus, an impulsion for doing something. Deriving from this difference between reason and result, there follows a difference in temporal orientation, such that a motive always looks to the future for its justification, whereas a motivation may sometimes stem from an event in the past. Compare (1) "Barger's motive for joining the club was his desire to improve his golf game" and (2) "Barger's motivation for joining the club (motivating him to join) lay in a friendly remark made by one of its members." One might substitute *motivation* in (1), although doing so would promote the role that was played by desire in arriving at the decision, that is, the temporal shading would be moved from the future into the past; but because of the orientation of *motive* toward the future, it could not replace *motivation* in (2).

nauseous/nauseated: *nausea* refers to a feeling of disgust or sickness to the stomach caused by something loathsome or offensive to the senses; *nauseous* is used of an object or situation that induces such a feeling; *nauseate* means "to induce or cause a feeling of nausea." The error to be guarded against in the use of these words is that of using *nauseous* in sentences like the following: "I feel nauseous," "It made me feel nauseous," and "The sight of the animal's mangled body made me nauseous." Expressions of this kind convey the (unintended) sense that the speaker is an object of the sort that causes nausea; compare "It made me feel disgusting," that is, as though I were something that caused disgust. What the speaker in such circumstances really means is expressed properly by "I was nauseated (by the sight)" or "It made me feel nauseated" or "The sight of the animal's mangled body nauseated me." The point is that *nauseous* is an adjective like *noxious, offensive, winning*, and the like, adjectives that project their semantic value toward the respondent. Their force does not lie in the attributing of a property to the speaker, as with adjectives like *happy, sad, willing*, say; it lies, rather, in the registering of a property of the speaker with the respondent. Thus, in saying "I feel (or "am") nauseous," the force of *nauseous* is shifted from the speaker onto the respondent, allowing for the unintended sense that the speaker is causing the interlocutor to feel nauseated.

negate/nullify: *negate* is properly used to impugn, deny, or reverse the truth claim made by a statement or assertion. It is thus imprecise to say (as is common) "That does not negate the fact that . . ." One does not negate facts. When what is being denied is the existence of some condition or state of affairs, the more appropriate word to use is *nullify;* thus, "Nothing in your argument nullifies (that is, renders null or inexistent) the fact that conditions in the mill were deplorable." The use of *negate* would be well motivated in a sentence like "Your opening statement negates (that is, repudiates, is in opposition to) the conclusion that you arrived at in your earlier article."

noisy/noisome: these two words are totally unrelated, both semantically and etymologically. *Noisy* derives ultimately from the Latin *nausea*, which meant "seasickness," whereas *noisome* goes back to a reduced (aphetic) form of *annoy* and means "offensive or disgusting," usually in connection with a smell or aroma. One can speak of a noisy sound or a noisome smell, but it is simply a mistake to use *noisome* when loud sounds or noises are in question.

nominate/denominate: both words mean "to name," but whereas *nominate* means "to call the name of," *denominate* means "to give a name to." In other words, only a person who has a name can be nominated, whereas denomination imposes no such requirement. In Eden, Adam denominated certain animals, calling one of them (by the word he used for) "tiger," another "lion," and so forth. After that, he could nominate them, that is, call them by name. In nominating, a name is invoked; in denominating, a person (or something) is labeled. Compare (1) "I nominate Doc Weinstein as president of the Wynnefield Boosters" and (2) "I denominate Doc Weinstein president of the Wynnefield Boosters." In (1), the doctor's name is invoked as that of a candidate to fill the post of president, but in (2), the doctor is named the president. Notice that in (2), although the doctor had a name, the post of president did not, and it is as the latter officer, that is, as president, that the doctor was denominated.

nominative absolute: recently gaining currency is an expression in which the word *absent* introduces a particular type of clause; exemplifying the usage are sentences like (1) "Absent a cut in the discount rate, the market will probably just drift for a while" and (2) "Absent a reprieve from the governor, execution of the prisoner will go forward as scheduled." If we construe the word *absent* as an adjective, it is not clear what grammatical construction we have in the opening clause(s). Some dictionaries include as a meaning for *absent* that of "lacking" and others list "without," but these meanings seem to be not so much grammatically motivated as to represent ad hoc concessions to the semantic function that *absent* performs in the clauses in question. In fact, the construction is that of a nominative absolute, that is, a clause in which a nominative element is modified by an adjective, noun, or participle, and where the resultant clause functions absolutely, meaning that it is not in grammatical construction with the main clause. In sentence (1), the nominative *cut* (in the noun phrase "a cut in the discount rate") is modified by *absent*, the entire clause functioning absolutely; in sentence (2), the nominative *reprieve* (in the noun phrase "a reprieve from the Governor") is similarly modified by *absent*.

The construction is common where the modifier is a participle: thus, "Given that all the conditions have been satisfied, we can now proceed with the transaction." Consider also a more complicated type: "It being understood that the second act is to be rewritten, we may proceed to order the costumes." An absolute construction that one hears with increasing frequency is one that begins "That aside," as in "That aside, I foresee no further problems." In this construction, *that* is the nominative and it is modified by the adjective *aside*; compare also the similar construction, "That said, we may go on to consider the remaining aspects of the problem."

Earlier I said that an absolute construction does not stand in a grammatical relation to the main clause of the sentence. This conclusion reduces to the fact that in such a construction the two clauses do not have a common subject, as in (1) and (2). This, however, is only a necessary condition for a construction to be absolute; it is not sufficient. Thus, consider the sentence "If there is no cut in the discount rate, the market will probably drift for a while." The respective subjects in the two clauses of this sentence are *cut* and *market*. But even though the clauses in this sentence employ different subjects, we do not have in the first clause an absolute construction; as is plain, it is simply a dependent clause.

none . . . is/are: compare (1) "None of the contestants is satisfied with the decision" and (2) "None of the contestants are satisfied with the decision." According to the rule that says that the verb must agree in number with the subject of the sentence, version

(1) is the correct form: *None* being singular ("no one"), agreement is achieved by *is*. However, version (2) is being used by more and more well-qualified speakers. The problem is caused, of course, by the fact that the noun closest to the verb in this construction is plural in number, and its proximity "attracts," as it were, the agreement to itself. The same problem is faced when the first element in the *of* phrase is a collective noun such as *group, body,* or *aggregate* and the verb is other than *be*; thus, we have "This group of players refuse/refuses to live at training camp." The lack of a clear-cut usage in this case is typical of a change in progress. That being the case, it would be linguistically anachronistic to condemn as totally unacceptable the secondary usage. (See the article on **attraction**.)

normalcy/normality: the English language would suffer little diminishment were *normalcy* to be stricken from its lexicon. The variant *normality* was no doubt formed on analogy with forms like *finality, banality, carnality, tonality*, and the like, that is, from underlying adjectives ending in *-al*. Its derivation is therefore consistent with that of its model(s). Addition of the suffix *-cy*, however, to form *normalcy*, would seem to be on analogy with nouns formed from underlying adjectives like *redundant, contingent, buoyant, expectant*, and the like, forms that yield the nouns *redundancy, contingency, buoyancy, expectancy*. In this case, therefore, the analogy is a false one, the forms taken as model(s) not being of a comparable structure. If I recall correctly, H. L. Mencken attributed the first use of *normalcy* to President Warren G. Harding, and commented in passing on its dubious credentials.

notable/noteworthy: consider the following sentence: (1) "Congress passed several noteworthy reforms in its last session; one of these reforms could in fact be called notable." What contrast is being suggested by the use of our two words in this sentence? In other words, if *noteworthy* means "worthy of note," what semantic feature is contributed by the meaning of *notable* that causes its use in (1) to be not redundant, but informative? It seems that to the meaning of *noteworthy*, the word *notable* adds the supplementary sense "because of some unusual or remarkable characteristic." A noteworthy career, say, would be one that in retrospect was found to merit notice; a notable career, by contrast, would be one that because of certain unusual or striking developments, had called attention to itself even as it was being realized.

numbers/numerals: numerals are symbols; numbers are the things that numerals symbolize. In the following sentences: "I saw 3 lambs in a meadow" and "I saw three lambs in a meadow," "3" and "three" are numerals. To be specific about what numbers are, however, is not altogether an easy task. Some people have held that numbers are things that really exist. Such people, as a rule, usually believe that such things as charity and forgiveness also exist. Others hold that numbers are concepts that we carry around in our minds and that numerals refer to those concepts. This is not the place to attempt a resolution of that problem, a problem that involves the nature of reality and the question of just what it is that words refer to. The purpose of this article is simply to indicate in a general way what the difference is between a numeral and a number.

oblige/obligate: both words mean "to place under a constraint," the difference in their meanings deriving from the weight or extent of the constraint in question—a heavier, more substantial kind motivating the use of *obligate*. In a sentence like "I was obliged to him," the constraint lying behind and motivating this sentence might be a favor or good turn in return for which I should be grateful; in "I was obligated to him," the constraint might be a loan in return for which I needed to perform some act. A friendly act might oblige me to someone; years of friendship would obligate me, place me under an obligation, to someone. One is as a rule obliged to people for something but is obligated by the law or by moral or religious principles to do something. Thus, "I'm obliged to my father for teaching me how to box," but "I'm obligated (by my religion) to obey my father." Consider a sentence like "Is the state obligated to help jurors return to normal lives?" If this sentence is intended to invite discussion on this question, it would seem to fail of its purpose, inasmuch as one could simply answer in the negative, there being no generally accepted legal, religious, or moral principle from which such an obligation might derive. But in the form "Is the state obliged to help jurors return to normal lives?" the sentence could very well lead to discussion, since now the emphasis is shifted to the fact that the jurors have rendered a service to the state, and it might justifiably be felt that something was due them in return. If I received an invitation to a party, I might feel obliged to reply; if I received a summons to jury duty, I would probably feel obligated to reply; the difference in word choice is a function of the different degrees of constraint that one would associate with the respective types of communication.

often/frequently: what difference in meaning is there between (1) "I often read in bed" and (2) "I frequently read in bed?" (1) simply suggests that I read in bed on a good many occasions, whereas (2) implies that the many occasions on which I read in bed occur fairly regularly and are separated by short intervals; no such inference about either regularity or length of interval is suggested by *often*. Compare now (3) "I don't often read fiction" and (4) "I don't frequently read fiction." Sentence (3) seems to deny that I read much fiction, whereas (4) implies that I read it now and again, only not regularly. In other words, in (3) the force of the negative is overriding in the interpretation of the sentence, whereas in (4), *frequently* retains its positive force. This difference probably derives from the fact that *frequently* has a denser semantic composition than does *often*, which does not have more in the way of meaning than a general sense of "many times."

on the part of/by: what is wrong with the following sentence? "There was a decidedly negative reaction on the part of Tebben to the dinner prepared for him by his wife." The sentence is representative of an inappropriate but increasingly more frequent use of *on the part of* when the simple *by* should be used. In the following sentence(s), the two expressions are properly used: (1) "There was a feeling on the part of those assembled that, perhaps, Lawrence had gone too far" (with any necessary syntactic modifications, *on the part of* would be used also with the following nouns: *sentiment, attitude, apprehension*) and (2) "There was a reaction by the assembled to Lawrence on account of his behavior" (*by* would also be used with the following nouns: *resistance, revulsion, opposition*). It seems that *on the part of* comports with the sentence(s) of (1) insofar as the noun describes a mental state and that *by* comports with the sentence(s) of (2) insofar as the noun describes a mental disposition. An even more questionable use of *on the part of* occurs in the following sentences: (3) "A decision was made on the part of the Republicans to stall the proceedings" and (4) "This action on the part of the Democrats served to stall the proceedings." When things are done, they are done by, not on the part of, people. In fact, in the latter sentence there is the slight intimation that the action was done for the benefit of the Democrats. In many of its uses, *on the part of* comes off simply as excess verbiage.

on/in behalf of: *on behalf of* is used when a person does something at the behest of someone else, *in behalf of* when a person does something for the benefit of someone (or something) else. In the first case a person is acting as a representative or spokesman for another party; in the second case the person is acting as an advocate or defender of such a party. Compare the sentences (1) "Wesley Monteith, the delegate from Pennsylvania, introduced a resolution on behalf of the steelworkers" and (2) "Wesley Monteith, the delegate from Pennsylvania, introduced a resolution in behalf of the steelworkers." In (1), Monteith has presumably been asked or commissioned to introduce the resolution, which may or may not involve him; in (2), Monteith may have acted not responsively but independently in introducing the resolution, which he thinks will benefit the steelworkers and which, again, may or may not involve him. In both cases, Monteith's introduction of the resolution is designed to benefit the steelworkers; the use of *on* or *in* (*behalf of*) is determined by whether Monteith's action in introducing the resolution followed a request or whether in introducing it he acted of his own volition. Compare, further, (3) "Monteith agreed to speak on the miners' behalf" and (4) "Monteith agreed to speak in the miners' behalf." In both sentences the inference is that Monteith agreed to speak for the miners. In (3), however, he speaks for them in the sense of speaking in their stead; in (4), he speaks for them in the sense of speaking for their benefit. In general, someone who acts in your behalf acts for you; someone who acts on your behalf acts instead of you.

ongoing/continuing: although there is a question as to the status of *ongoing* as a legitimate English word, I will for the moment overlook its dubious credentials and adduce some considerations that might bear on a semantic distinction between its use and that of the word *continuing*. In *ongoing*, the semantic emphasis is on the fact that the process occurs without interruption; in *continuing*, on the fact that it is projected forward in time. Compare (1) "The investigation is ongoing" with (2) "The investigation is continuing." The former sentence describes the investigation as though it were a bounded exercise, a fixed state of affairs; but if one were to say (3) "This investigation is (has been) an ongoing one," there would be an intimation of a contrast with an investigation that has suffered interruption. Substitution of *continuing* for *ongoing* in either (1) or (3) would introduce an implication of open-endedness in the investigation, a projection of its tenure into the future. With *ongoing*, there is additionally the suggestion of a punctuality, a momentaneousness, a suggestion that is not necessarily imparted by *continuing*; compare (4) "At this time we join the ongoing discussion of city finances." In this sentence the temporal value of *ongoing* consists with the punctuality of *at this time*; however, use of *contin-*

uing in (4) would produce a discord between the sense of "presentness" conveyed by *at this time* and the extension into the future suggested by *continuing*.

or: the reviewer of a recent book commented, (1) "[the book] is organized as a series of linked vignettes: after 10 pages, you can take time out to hug your child, call a friend, stroll in the sun." Noteworthy about this sentence is the absence of *or* before the last alternative in the series of disjuncts that ends the sentence. Normally, we would expect such a sentence to read (2) ". . . you can take time out to hug your child, call a friend, or stroll in the sun." In omitting the conjunction in (1), the reviewer introduces a significant shading on how the sentence is to be understood. A sequence in which the last in a series of alternatives is preceded by *or* presents the alternatives as exhausting the range of possibilities, whereas one in which the *or* is omitted suggests that the possibilities are not so limited—that others exist beyond those that have been mentioned. Compare (3) "In the evening, I read, write, or go to the movies." This sentence suggests that my evenings are spent pursuing one of the three activities mentioned here. In (4), however, "In the evening, I read, write, go to the movies," the possibility is left open that I may pursue some activity not mentioned in the series. In sentences like (2) and (4) in which the *or* is omitted, one almost feels that the voice's intonation does not drop, as it would with the *or*, but that it remains level, implying that there are more alternatives to come. It is as though the sentence were written "In the evening, I read, write, go to the movies . . . "

orient/orientate: as verbs, both these forms mean "to position or align with respect to the (eastern) surroundings." As to their derivations, the form *orient* is probably the result of a functional shift (which see) from the noun *orient*, and *orientate* is probably a back-formation (which see) from the noun *orientation*. In terms of derivational lineage, therefore, *orient* has a better pedigree. It is preferable also from another standpoint. A Hindu grammarian once said that he would rather save a mora (roughly a syllable) in his analysis of Sanskrit phonology than father a son. Not everyone will feel this strongly about syllabic economy, but anything that will reduce the amount of phonetic surfeit in the atmosphere is to be recommended. Say *orient.*

parameter/perimeter: a parameter is a constant whose value (perhaps along with the values of other constants) serves to determine the characteristics or the behavior of some variable; thus, protein content might be one of the parameters determining the nutritional value of certain foods, or the neighborhood and the school system might be among the parameters determining the value of the local real estate; a perimeter is simply the boundary delimiting a certain area. Thus, the suburbs of a city occur at its perimeter; the fences in a baseball stadium form part of the playing field's perimeter. In general, a parameter serves to define or identify, a perimeter to bound or enclose.

pare/peel: as a rule, paring is done with a knife, peeling with the fingers; we pare the skins of apples but peel those of oranges. Grapes, having skins that are comparatively delicate, require peeling only for palates of extreme refinement. It is not, however, only fruits that may be subjected to these trimming procedures. And here again discrimination is required in the application of our two words; thus, we pare (down) costs and we peel (off) clothing; we pare (down) expenses and we peel (off) dollar bills.

part/portion: a portion is a part of something regarded as belonging to or pertaining to a person; thus, a pie may be divided into parts, but each such part, when offered to a person, becomes a portion, in other words, the part allotted to that person. The part of the common wealth that a woman brings to a marriage is regarded as her portion (her dowry). The part of the general destiny that God allots to a person is regarded as that person's portion.

participle/gerund: consider the following sentences: "I distinctly remember my uncle/uncle's telling me that the earth is flat," "The thought of the cat/cat's purring somehow comforted him," "I couldn't recall anyone/anyone's raising an objection to the plan." The grammatical crux embodied in these sentences devolves upon a noun and a following *-ing* form (viz., "uncle/uncle's telling," "cat/cat's purring," "anyone/anyone's raising"). In these constructions, it turns out that when the noun is in the common case, the *-ing* form functions as a (present) participle, and when it is in the possessive case, the *-ing* form functions as a gerund. Although both forms of construction are grammatically correct, a subtle difference in "emphasis" results from the use of one or the other of these two constructions. With the common case of the noun (and the correlative participle), the emphasis is on the noun; with the possessive case of the noun (and the correlative gerund), the emphasis is on the gerund. In other words, the different grammatical constructions cause us to focus our attention, respectively, on the agent (uncle, cat, anyone) or on the activity (telling, purring, raising). To return to our first example "I remember my uncle/uncle's telling me that the earth is flat," in the first version (with *telling* functioning as a participle), what I remember primarily is *my uncle* as he is telling me that the earth is flat; in the second version (with *telling* functioning as a gerund), what I remember primarily is my uncle's *telling* me that the earth is flat.

partly/partially: compare (1) "The lake is partly frozen" and (2) "The lake is partially frozen." The inference from (1) is that only a part of the lake's area is frozen, from (2) that the lake's material (i.e., its water) is to some extent frozen. Sentence (1) would be consistent with there being pools of water on the lake's frozen surface, (2) when there are no such pools but certain slushy areas on the lake's surface instead. Compare also (3) "Paul's argument is partly correct" and (4) "Paul's argument is partially correct." From (3), the inference is that parts of Paul's argument are valid; from (4), that his argument (as a whole) has some merit. In construction with a predicate, *partly* reduces the *extent* of the predicate's effect, and *partially* reduces the *application* of the predicate's effect.

peaceful/peaceable: *peaceful* means "characterized by peace, in a state of peace"; *peaceable* means "disposed toward peace, inclined toward peace." Compare (1) "The neighborhood is now peaceable" and (2) "The neighborhood is now peaceful." Sentence (1) would be appropriate if after a period of ethnic or racial strife, a softening of attitude had set in and the various sides in the dispute were now ready to discuss measures designed to ease tension; sentence (2) would be appropriate if discussions had in fact taken place and calm had been restored to the neighborhood. Compare now (3) "After a period of extreme agony, the patient had ceased his moaning and was finally peaceful" and (4) "After a period of extreme bellicosity, the patient had ceased his ranting and had turned peaceable." The exchange of *peaceful* and *peaceable* in these two sentences would render each one semantically dubious; justification for such uses could perhaps be provided, but it would entail recourse to senses of the words that were motivated in the first place precisely by inexact uses of the sort that the exchange would represent (presence of a sense in a dictionary may permit a use but it does not necessarily justify it). In general, it seems that it is people (or collectivities of people—neighborhoods, nations, societies, and so forth) that have the ability to be peaceable, whereas it is states of affairs or conditions that can be peaceful.

perceptive/percipient: the use of these two words may be distinguished on the basis that *percipient* functions to describe a characteristic of a person, whereas in addition to being used in this function, *perceptive* may also be used to characterize an observation, an analysis, a piece of criticism, and so forth. In other words, activities of various sorts that would not support the predicate *percipient* may be termed "perceptive." In choosing between (1) "That was a very perceptive analysis" and (2) "That was a very percipient analysis," we would choose (1) if we wished the focus to fall on the analysis and (2) if we wished it to fall on the analyzer.

permeate/pervade/penetrate: the difference between permeation and pervasion is that the former process affects a surface, the latter an area; however, it is characteristic of penetration that it is effected upon a solid substance. A liquid or a gas, say, will permeate a film or a membrane, by passing through the pores or interstices thereof, whereas a voice, an odor, or a fragrance will pervade a room or a house. Penetration, in addition to being effected upon solid substances, is also effected by such. Knives, daggers, and nails are some of the more common penetrants. Compare now (1) "The coffee permeated Acie Crawford's leather jacket" and (2) "The dagger penetrated Acie Crawford's leather jacket." The coffee in (1) will have passed *into* the jacket and spread throughout it; the dagger in (2) will have passed *through* the jacket and reached beyond it. Moreover, the knife will have pervaded the area into which it has reached; it will have penetrated Acie Crawford's skin and pervaded his flesh. To say of coffee that it has pervaded something, it would be necessary that there be an open space (an area) into which the coffee has run—the space, however, would have to be large. Thus, under certain circumstances, we could say that coffee pervaded the dishwasher, but it would be hard to imagine circumstances under which we would say that it pervaded a cup.

perquisite/prerequisite: the problem raised by this pair is not a function of semantic affinity, as the meanings are quite disparate, *perquisite* meaning a fringe benefit associated with a position or occupation and *prerequisite* meaning a preliminary condition associated with a post or occupation. What might cause a problem, of course, is the near correspondence in spelling. In the following sentences the words are used correctly: "A perquisite of Harley's job was a season's box at the opera" and "A prerequisite for the job with the insurance company was a knowledge of Japanese." (Notice how the prepositions *of* and *for* correlate with our two words.) *Perquisite* occurs as a clipped form, namely, *perk*: "Of the many perks associated with his new position, Denny appreciated most the private shower."

perspicuous/perspicacious: in general, we say of a thing that it is perspicuous, of a person that he or she is perspicacious. Perspicuity is a property of an object, a product, or design; perspicacity is a faculty that enables a person to see clearly into the nature of a problem or situation. Therefore, a text, an argument, an explanation may be perspicuous, but it is the person analyzing or seeing into these constructions who is perspicacious. The same object—say, an analysis or a piece of reasoning—may sometimes be termed either perspicuous or perspicacious, depending on whether we approach it as a product or a process. Words like *analysis* and *reasoning,* say, lend themselves to this product/process ambiguity; compare (1) "His analysis (reasoning) was perspicuous/perspicacious." With *perspicuous,* the focus is on the analysis as finished product; with *perspicacious,* it is on the analyzing process itself. The meaning of a word like *argument* in a context like that of (1) will assume the sense of product if paired with *perspicuous* and that of process when paired with *perspicacious.* In similar fashion, a word like *reasoning* in a context like (1) will vary in function between that of a gerund or a present participle depending on whether it occurs with *perspicuous* or *perspicacious.*

persuade/convince: to persuade is to get someone to do something; to convince is to get someone to think something. Persuading typically leads to action; convincing leads to thought. It is interesting that the nominal derived from *persuade* is *persuasion,* which refers to a form of activity, whereas *conviction,* the nominal associated with *convince,* describes a mental state. Compare now (1) "Ms. Harper persuaded Benson to look for a new job" and (2) "Ms. Harper convinced Benson (of the fact) that he should look for a new job." The pragmatic distinction described here is reflected in the syntactic difference displayed by these two sentences. Further, it appears that in persuading Benson, Ms. Harper would be giving reasons, whereas in convincing him, she would be offering arguments. By way of persuading Benson, Ms. Harper might point to his poor sales record, his chronic lateness, or his insubordinate attitude; by way of convincing him, she might point to the general falling off of the company's annual sales, its new policy of advancing only minority workers, or its pending move to Europe. Consider now a passive version of these sentences: (3) "Benson was persuaded that his future lay elsewhere" and (4) "Benson was convinced that his future lay elsewhere." There is the sense in (3) that the persuasion was performed upon Benson by someone other than himself, whereas (4) is ambiguous, that is, it may mean that someone convinced him that his future lay elsewhere, but it may also be interpreted to mean that Benson had become convinced, that is, now had the conviction, that his future lay elsewhere. It is true that sentence (3) also allows for this adjectival reading (of *persuaded*), but that reading appears to be the result of the usage "I was persuaded (in the sense of "I was certain") that . . . ," a usage that has an air of the nouveau about it. Bearing further on this subtle distinction is the fact that the construction "I became convinced that . . ." is an acceptable formulation, whereas "I became persuaded that . . ." poses a certain awkwardness for its processor.

phenomenon/phenomena: it is not clear why an article should be necessary about the usage of these forms, but apparently it is. Many speakers, including quite a few of substantial educational attainments, use the form *phenomena* as a singular, in sentences like the following, for example: (1) "Will this be the end of the Irabu phenomena?" or (2) "This phenomena is becoming increasingly more prevalent," or (3) "We are witnessing a phenomena that will have grave consequences for the future of the arts." In sentence (1), even though it is extremely unlikely that it was the speaker's intent, it would be possible to rationalize the use of the plural form on the basis that there was more than one phenomenon associated with Hideki Irabu (the Yankee pitcher). In sentences (2) and (3), however, the use of the plural form is a flat-out mistake, and it is a mistake not infrequently heard. *Phenomenon* is one of a handful of words borrowed from the Greek that form their plurals with the ending *-a* (*criterion, rhododendron,* *anacoluthon, enchiridion* are a few of the others). When these words are used in the singular, the form to be used is of course the form ending with *-on*. (Recently overheard: "Credit criteria has tightened a bit in the last six months," where the use of *has* shows that the speaker takes *criteria* to be singular.)

place to visit/place to relax: compare the following sentences: (1) "Niagara Falls is a nice place to visit," (2) "A bird call is a pleasant sound to hear," (3) "A lottery is a good prize to win," (4) "The bathtub is a pleasant place to relax," (5) "General Motors is an excellent place to work," and (6) "A sandbox is a good place to play." Sentences (1–3) represent correct uses, whereas a question may be raised about sentences (4–6). The difference in our reactions is a function of the differing underlying structures of the two types of sentences. Suppose that we supply a subject for the final verbs in these sentences. If we supply such a subject, sentence (1) becomes something like (1a) "Niagara Falls is a nice place for someone (or, for a person) to visit" and (4) becomes something like (4a) "The bathtub is a pleasant place for someone (or, for a person) to relax." But whereas (1a) strikes us as quite satisfactory, (4a) seems somewhat unfinished or incomplete; it would seem more satisfactory if rounded off somehow as (4b): "The bathtub is a pleasant place for someone (or, for a person) to relax in." This suggests that an improved form for sentences (4–6) would be one that added a preposition at the end. Another factor that serves to promote the different responses to sentences of the two types— reckoning one type grammatically acceptable but the other type questionable—is that the type represented by (1–3) ends in a transitive verb, whereas the type represented by (4–6) ends in an intransitive verb. This fact is significant in that the verbs engage the subject nouns in sentences (1–3) but leave them, without the added prepositions, "unengaged" in sentences (4–6).

pleaded/pled: both forms are acceptable as the past tense of *plead*. Although the etymologically more legitimate variant is no doubt *pled,* a word or two concerning that form's probable genesis might be in order. In Old English, certain weak verbs that ended in the dental consonants (*d* or *t*) doubled those consonants and added a vowel in forming their past tenses—thus, *readde, fedde, gette,* and so on. Although *plead* was borrowed from Old French only during the Middle English period, it apparently underwent the same treatment on its entry into English—namely, *pleadde.* The final vowel (of these dissyllabic forms) was subsequently lost and the doubled consonants simplified, leaving us today with such past tense forms as *led, fed, read, set,* and so forth. *Pled* is probably such a form, simplified in its spelling from *plead,* which itself could be used as a past tense form, that is, we could write "The prisoner plead guilty" (cf. *read*). The form *pleaded* is then a reformulated past tense, one accorded the full past suffix.

plenitude/plenty: compare (1) "At the offices of the Society to Combat World Poverty, there was a plenitude of compassion, altruism, and good will; such things as food, clothing, and cash, however, were not there in plenty." An inference from our use of the two words in (1) would be that *plenitude* is indicated when the amount in question is of something abstract, whereas concrete amounts motivate a use of *plenty.* In line with this hypothesis we would conclude that sentences (2) "Rose petals were strewn in plenty along the garden paths" and (3) "Her mind was assailed by a plenitude of unpleasant memories" are correctly worded. As synonyms of *plenitude,* we have words like *abundance* and *copiousness;* synonymous with *plenty* might be the more concrete *large supply.*

practical/pragmatic: the sense in question here is that relating to a particular attitude taken by individuals toward their everyday affairs, one that is prosaic, concrete, unimaginative. In this connection the essential difference between the two terms is that *practical* applies when what is in question is the *conduct* of these affairs, whereas *pragmatic* applies when the question is the *planning* with respect to these affairs. So that "Axie is a practical person" suggests a person who is efficient in the carrying out, the actual performance, of her everyday affairs, whereas "Axie is a pragmatic person" suggests that she thinks carefully about, reflects methodically on, the most efficient way to carry out those affairs.

precipitous/precipitate: the adjective *precipitous* derives from *precipice* and, as that word refers to a vertical cliff or the sharp falling-off of a mountain, so *precipitous* describes something that is steep or sharply falling off. Thus, a precipitous drop is a sudden, steep drop, a precipitous decline is a sharp, sudden decline, say in a road or path. The adjective *precipitate*, however, is derived from the verb *to precipitate*, which refers to a *process*, a process in which something takes place suddenly or abruptly, a process in which something is *precipitated*; and the adjective incorporates this component of meaning. Thus, a precipitate decision, a precipitate resolution, would be a decision and a resolution arrived at hastily, without any thought or deliberation. As is suggested by the examples, *precipitous* is used in relation to physical or natural objects, *precipitate* in relation to human actions or processes. One would not refer to a judgment as precipitous or to a judgment as having been arrived at precipitously; by the same token, one would not refer to a precipitate ski run or to a ski run as dropping off precipitately.

predilection/propensity: a propensity is a tendency; a predilection is a partiality. Thus, a propensity is a behavioral predisposition (a person has a propensity to do something or other), whereas a predilection is a personal characteristic (a person has a predilection for something or other). Compare (1) "Dudley has a propensity to speak before thinking" and (2) "Dudley has a predilection for speaking before thinking." Sentence (1) suggests that in speaking before thinking Dudley is obeying an inclination that he has; sentence (2) suggests that in doing so Dudley is indulging a preference of his. (Notice how the prepositions *to* and *for* correlate respectively with *propensity* and *predilection*.)

presently/at present: *presently* means "shortly"; *at present* means "at the time of speaking." One can therefore say "At present it would be premature to answer that question" (or "It would be premature to answer that question at present") and "The answer to that question will be provided presently" (or "Presently, the answer . . . "). It would be a usage misdemeanor, however (if not, in fact, a crime), to say "Presently, it would be premature to answer that question."

presumably/putatively: the difference in meaning between these two words may be understood as representing a difference between how something appears to a person and how it appears to the world, or between what a person supposes of a thing and what the world attributes to it. Consider (1) "The new model presumably represented a breakthrough in automotive design" and (2) "The new model putatively represented a breakthrough in automotive design." Sentence (1) may be paraphrased as (3) "Someone (or people collectively) think or suppose that the new model represents a breakthrough in automotive design." A paraphrase of (2) would go something like (4) "It is imputed of the new model that it represents a breakthrough in automotive design." Compare now (5a/b): "The aerodynamic design is a presumed/putative advantage of the new model." Sentence (5a) suggests that in the opinion of people, the design is considered an advantage, whereas (5b) implies that an opinion of people that the design is an advantage has been attributed to the new model.

preterition: an interesting figure of thought in which the speaker disclaims the intention to say something that is said in the very disclaimer (most dictionaries do not offer such a definition for the word; in order to find this type of definition, it is necessary

he has; sentence (2) suggests that in doing so Dudley is
g a preference of his. (Notice how the prepositions *to*
correlate respectively with *propensity* and *predilection*.)

at present: *presently* means "shortly"; *at present* means
time of speaking." One can therefore say "At present it
e premature to answer that question" (or "It would be
re to answer that question at present") and "The an-
that question will be provided presently" (or "Presently,
ver . . . "). It would be a usage misdemeanor, however (if
act, a crime), to say "Presently, it would be premature to
that question."

ly/putatively: the difference in meaning between these
rds may be understood as representing a difference be-
ow something appears to a person and how it appears to
ld, or between what a person supposes of a thing and
e world attributes to it. Consider (1) "The new model
ably represented a breakthrough in automotive design"
"The new model putatively represented a breakthrough
motive design." Sentence (1) may be paraphrased as (3)
ne (or people collectively) think or suppose that the new
represents a breakthrough in automotive design." A
ase of (2) would go something like (4) "It is imputed of
y model that it represents a breakthrough in automotive
" Compare now (5a/b): "The aerodynamic design is a
ed/putative advantage of the new model." Sentence (5a)
s that in the opinion of people, the design is considered
antage, whereas (5b) implies that an opinion of people
e design is an advantage has been attributed to the new

n: an interesting figure of thought in which the speaker
ns the intention to say something that is said in the very
ner (most dictionaries do not offer such a definition for
rd; in order to find this type of definition, it is necessary

anacoluthon, enchiridion are a few of the others). When these
words are used in the singular, the form to be used is of course
the form ending with -*on*. (Recently overheard: "Credit criteria
has tightened a bit in the last six months," where the use of *has*
shows that the speaker takes *criteria* to be singular.)

place to visit/place to relax: compare the following sentences: (1)
"Niagara Falls is a nice place to visit," (2) "A bird call is a
pleasant sound to hear," (3) "A lottery is a good prize to win,"
(4) "The bathtub is a pleasant place to relax," (5) "General Motors is an excellent place to work," and (6) "A sandbox is a
good place to play." Sentences (1–3) represent correct uses,
whereas a question may be raised about sentences (4–6). The
difference in our reactions is a function of the differing underlying structures of the two types of sentences. Suppose that we
supply a subject for the final verbs in these sentences. If we supply such a subject, sentence (1) becomes something like (1a)
"Niagara Falls is a nice place for someone (or, for a person) to
visit" and (4) becomes something like (4a) "The bathtub is a
pleasant place for someone (or, for a person) to relax." But
whereas (1a) strikes us as quite satisfactory, (4a) seems somewhat unfinished or incomplete; it would seem more satisfactory
if rounded off somehow as (4b): "The bathtub is a pleasant
place for someone (or, for a person) to relax in." This suggests
that an improved form for sentences (4–6) would be one that
added a preposition at the end. Another factor that serves to
promote the different responses to sentences of the two types—
reckoning one type grammatically acceptable but the other type
questionable—is that the type represented by (1–3) ends in a
transitive verb, whereas the type represented by (4–6) ends in an
intransitive verb. This fact is significant in that the verbs engage
the subject nouns in sentences (1–3) but leave them, without the
added prepositions, "unengaged" in sentences (4–6).

pleaded/pled: both forms are acceptable as the past tense of *plead*.
Although the etymologically more legitimate variant is no doubt

pled, a word or two concerning that form's probable genesis might be in order. In Old English, certain weak verbs that ended in the dental consonants (*d* or *t*) doubled those consonants and added a vowel in forming their past tenses—thus, *readde, fedde, gette*, and so on. Although *plead* was borrowed from Old French only during the Middle English period, it apparently underwent the same treatment on its entry into English—namely, *pleadde*. The final vowel (of these dissyllabic forms) was subsequently lost and the doubled consonants simplified, leaving us today with such past tense forms as *led, fed, read, set*, and so forth. *Pled* is probably such a form, simplified in its spelling from *plead*, which itself could be used as a past tense form, that is, we could write "The prisoner plead guilty" (cf. *read*). The form *pleaded* is then a reformulated past tense, one accorded the full past suffix.

plenitude/plenty: compare (1) "At the offices of the Society to Combat World Poverty, there was a plenitude of compassion, altruism, and good will; such things as food, clothing, and cash, however, were not there in plenty." An inference from our use of the two words in (1) would be that *plenitude* is indicated when the amount in question is of something abstract, whereas concrete amounts motivate a use of *plenty*. In line with this hypothesis we would conclude that sentences (2) "Rose petals were strewn in plenty along the garden paths" and (3) "Her mind was assailed by a plenitude of unpleasant memories" are correctly worded. As synonyms of *plenitude*, we have words like *abundance* and *copiousness*; synonymous with *plenty* might be the more concrete *large supply*.

practical/pragmatic: the sense in question here is that relating to a particular attitude taken by individuals toward their everyday affairs, one that is prosaic, concrete, unimaginative. In this connection the essential difference between the two terms is that *practical* applies when what is in question is the *conduct* of

these affairs, whereas *pragmati[c] planning* with respect to these [ ] cal person" suggests a person [ ] out, the actual performance, [ ] "Axie is a pragmatic person" s[ ] about, reflects methodically on[ ] out those affairs.

precipitous/precipitate: the adje[ ] *precipice* and, as that word refe[ ] falling-off of a mountain, so *p[ ]* that is steep or sharply falling o[ ] sudden, steep drop, a precipitou[ ] cline, say in a road or path. Th[ ] is derived from the verb *to preci[ ]* a process in which something ta[ ] a process in which something is [ ] incorporates this component of [ ] cision, a precipitate resolution, [ ] lution arrived at hastily, without [ ] is suggested by the examples, *pr[ ]* physical or natural objects, *prec[ ]* tions or processes. One would n[ ] itous or to a judgment as having [ ] by the same token, one would n[ ] or to a ski run as dropping off pr[ ]

predilection/propensity: a propensit[ ] is a partiality. Thus, a propensity [ ] (a person has a propensity to do s[ ] predilection is a personal characte[ ] tion for something or other). [ ] propensity to speak before thin[ ] predilection for speaking before th[ ] that in speaking before thinking [ ]

tion th[ ] indulg[ ] and *fo[ ]*

presently[ ] "at the [ ] would [ ] prema[ ] swer to [ ] the ans[ ] not, in [ ] answer[ ]

presuma[ ] two w[ ] tween [ ] the w[ ] what [ ] presum[ ] and (2[ ] in aut[ ] "Some[ ] model [ ] parap[ ] the ne[ ] design[ ] presu[ ] sugge[ ] an ad[ ] that t[ ] mode[ ]

preteri[ ] discla[ ] discla[ ] the w[ ]

to consult a handbook of rhetorical terms, where the figure may be listed under *preterition* or under its Greek name, *apophasis*). Office seekers find in preterition a very useful device, in that they can bring to an audience's attention the most damaging features of their opponent's position and background and at the same time present themselves as too principled to be actually indulging in mudslinging. The following might be considered a representative sample: "I intend to conduct this campaign on a respectable level. Thus, I will not refer to my opponent's divorce, the suits that have been brought against him for nonpayment of alimony, his having been in jail several times on the charge of driving while impaired. No, I will not stoop to such a level. As I said, I intend to conduct this campaign on a higher level."

preternatural/supernatural: both words signify a state or condition that surpasses the bounds of the natural, but *preternatural* (Lat. *praeter,* "beyond") indicates that this outstripping of the natural is a matter of degree, whereas *supernatural* (Lat. *super,* "above") indicates that it is a matter of kind. Therefore, a sparrow that weighed one hundred pounds or a snowfall that lasted twenty-five days would be preternatural phenomena, whereas a goblin of any height or the spontaneous appearance of Elvis Presley in the sky (that is, the appearance of the actual Elvis, not a likeness of him in a cloud or star formation) would represent the supernatural.

prevent/preclude: the meanings of these two words overlap to some extent, but there are contexts in which only one of them is appropriate. In sentences like (1) "Jim was prevented by his brother from leaving the house" or (2) "Jim prevented his sister from going to graduate school," the word *preclude* would be inappropriate. Conversely, *prevent* would be inappropriate in sentences like (3) "Charles Kenny was precluded from practicing law by his failure to pass the bar exam" and (4) "The care with which the experiment was carried out precluded any possibility of error." As these sentences illustrate, in those contexts where *prevent* means "to stop" and is an act performed or a condition imposed by a person, *preclude* is inappropriate, whereas in those contexts in which *preclude* means "to rule out" and where this ruling out is a consequence of some condition or state of affairs, it would be inappropriate to use *prevent*. There are, to be sure, contexts in which a nonhuman agency may be the subject of *prevent*; compare "The strong tides prevented the ship from mooring"; the converse case, however, is apparently not acceptable, namely, "The guard precluded the students from entering the hall."

previous/preceding: both words mean "occurring before the time of their utterance," but *preceding* adds the component "immediately." A sentence said to have occurred previously in a text, say, may have occurred anywhere in that text prior to the sentence in which *previous* occurs, but reference to a preceding sentence specifies the sentence just before the one in which *preceding* occurs. As a corollary of this difference there will as a rule be associated with *previous* the indefinite article, whereas with *preceding* it will be the definite article: Thus, one will speak of "a previous" but of "the preceding" sentence.

privilege/prerogative: on the occasion of President Clinton's exercise of the line-item veto, the event was described by a TV announcer in the following manner: "The president has just applied the line-item veto to the balanced budget agreement. President Clinton is the first president that has had that privilege." The word that would more appropriately have marked the significance of the occasion and the exclusiveness of the right exercised is "prerogative." Both a privilege and a prerogative are special rights accorded to certain people, but whereas a privilege is a right that may be extended to a group or a number of people, a prerogative is a right that, customarily, is vested in a single person. Thus, every member of Congress has the right (is privileged) to offer an amendment to a bill, but no member of

Congress has as a prerogative the right to veto a bill; that is a power residing exclusively with the president, a person for whom it is a prerogative.

proactive: a word of dubious etymological credentials currently pushing its way into the common speech. Consider the following sentence, recently overheard: "I'm a very proactive lawyer, in the sense that I want to get all the information out there." What is the use of "proactive" supposed to convey here that would not be conveyed by "active," or "diligent," or "conscientious," or a host of other words that would more precisely describe what this lawyer regards as a strong suit in the conduct of cases? The answer, of course, is "buzz." But the morphological background of this form is decidedly shady. The adverbial form *pro* may be prefixed to words like *union, animal rights, school integration, tax cuts,* and other such forms to indicate being in favor of those causes; and, of course, it figures in a host of Latin and Greek derivations in which, originally as a prefix, it modified the sense of some stem or other (cf. *produce, proclaim, propel,* and many other such). But what is that element doing in *proactive?* Does it mean that one is in favor of being active—what, rather than passive? Why would this claim need to be made? Is it supposed to pair off with *reactive?* But this state is taken care of by the simple *active.* If it is supposed to pair off with *retroactive,* the form, I should think, would be *preactive.* As far as I can see, the use of this word is simply another example of the deplorable tendency to jump on and spread a usage that some speaker, in a stroke of lexical or morphological bravado, saw fit to perpetrate upon a defenseless language.

process/procedure: a process is a set or series of actions directed to some end; a procedure is an act or manner of proceeding in a given action or process. A procedure is therefore one of the actions in the set of actions that constitute a process. In the process of running for legislative office, for example, one of the procedures would be that of filing notice of one's candidacy.

prognosis/prognostication: both words have the meaning "forecast or prediction," primarily with reference to the future course to be taken by a sickness or disease; the difference in their meanings derives largely from the fact that *prognostication*, by virtue of its having been derived from the verbal *prognosticate*, contains in its meaning a sense of the actual proffering of a forecast or making of a prediction, a sense that is lacking from the meaning of *prognosis*. Because of this shade of difference in the respective meanings, a patient suffering from a particular disease might ask the doctor either "What is the prognosis for this disease?" or "What is your prognostication for my condition?" (or "What prognostication do you make for my recovery from this disease?"). Both forms of the question would be appropriate. In the former case, the question refers to the general medical opinion about the course of the disease; in the latter it refers to the doctor's opinion about the recovery chances of the particular patient. The contrast is exemplified in the following statement that a doctor might make to a patient: "The general prognosis for this condition is that it requires a long period of convalescence; my (personal) prognostication, however, is that you'll be up and around in a couple of weeks."

prolix/verbose: both words mean "using a surfeit of words." The difference is that *prolix* is used when the surfeit in question is viewed as a property of a person's manner of speaking or writing; *verbose* is used when the surfeit is regarded as a personal characteristic of that speaker, thus, when the impression of excessiveness is attributed not to the language product but to the processor of that product. Compare the following sentences: (1) "I find reading Thackeray very tiring; his style is so prolix" and (2) "I can't discuss anything with Harry for very long; he is so verbose."

proportional/proportionate: the words are used properly in the following sentences: (1) "Eddie Kernish arranged for a proportionate division of the proceeds," (2) "Each member of the championship team received a proportionate share of the bonus money," (3) "The share of the proceeds given to Sunstein was proportional to the share given to Pearsall," and (4) "The amount of time that Kligie spent on his financial affairs was proportional to the amount he spent on leisure activities." The first thing to notice is that whereas *proportionate* functions as an attributive adjective, *proportional* functions as a predicate adjective: In (1) and (2), *proportionate* modifies an element that figures in a relation of proportionality; in (3) and (4), *proportional* connects elements that stand in such a relation.

propound/propose: both words mean "to set forth for consideration," but *propound* is used when the setting forth is more extensive, more substantial, more highly developed. In general, one would propound a plan but propose an idea. In propounding a project, say, one sets out in some detail the elements of the project; in proposing a project, one need merely state what it is. Compare "It took McAleer fifteen minutes to propound his scheme for the new curriculum" and "McAleer proposed one scheme after another for the new curriculum." In propounding, one sets out a proposal; in proposing, one makes a proposal. In propounding a project, the speaker's interest is in the project; in proposing a project, the speaker's interest is in its acceptance.

proprietary/proprietorial: the dictionary will provide for *proprietary* the meanings both "pertaining to ownership" and "pertaining to property." For the former meaning, however, the form *proprietorial*, with its basis in *proprietor*, is to be preferred. A sentence like "Most of the workers in that factory take a proprietary interest in its success" poses an ambiguity in that it may be read as meaning (1) that the workers were interested in the factory's success because it would benefit the factory or as meaning (2) that they were interested because it would benefit themselves. The ambiguity is unavoidable if (1) is the intended meaning; however, reading (2) may be rendered unambiguously with the use of *proprietorial*.

purposely/purposefully: both adverbs function to modify the meaning of verbs, with *purposely* adding the sense "deliberately, intentionally," *purposefully* adding the sense "having some object, goal, or end in mind." Compare (1) "Arnold Koffler strode purposely into the conference room" and (2) "Arnold Koffler strode purposefully into the conference room." In (1), Koffler made a deliberate point of walking into the conference room, whereas in (2), he walked into the room with the intention to accomplish a particular purpose.

question/query: a query differs from a question in that it suggests a reservation or disagreement. This means that a query usually occurs in a situation where information has already been provided. A query, thus, asks not so much for information as it does for ampli- or clarification. Thus, although I might question you about how you had settled with your neighbor over his complaint about the noise coming from your apartment, I could not very well query you on that subject; but after you had given me an answer, I could query you about why you had settled the complaint in just that way. Or consider (1) "Willis questioned his supervisor about the work schedule for the following day" and (2) "Willis queried his supervisor about the work schedule for the following day." Sentence (1) would be appropriate if Willis had not yet seen the work schedule, whereas (2) implies that Willis has seen it and, not being clear or satisfied about certain of its details, is asking for clarification or justification.

quote/quotation: a sentence like the following incorporates a common error: (1) "I just came across a beautiful quote that I can use in my promotional campaign." Although some dictionaries assign a noun function to *quote* and thus would permit a use like that in (1), the assignment, in my opinion, should be taken not so much as representing a sanction for such a use but rather as constituting a surrender to a common misuse. One should use *quote* exclusively as a verb and use *quotation* when a noun is indicated.

racial/racist: as adjectives, these two forms have quite dissimilar meanings. Compare (1) "There was an obvious racial component in the campaign" and (2) "There was an obvious racist component in the campaign." Sentence (1) might be used to describe a campaign in which candidates of different races were running for office, whereas sentence (2) would be used to describe a campaign in which charges or comments had been made that impugned the characters or disparaged the abilities of some candidates on the basis of their race. *Racial* is essentially a descriptive term; *racist*, however, is a term that is connotatively supercharged. A remark "with racist overtones" is one whose meaning lies not so much in what was said as in what was implied or suggested by what was said, where what was implied or suggested is inimical or disadvantageous to a particular race.

rationale/rationalization: both forms signify an explanation in which reasons are given for the propriety of beliefs or behavior, but whereas the reasons given in a rationale are presumed to be objective and disinterested, those given in a rationalization tend to be biased and to serve the speaker's self-interest. In many cases, a rationale is given for a future course of action, whereas a rationalization is offered for a past action. One would provide a rationale in trying to convince someone of the feasibility or desirability of a project; one would offer a rationalization as a measure of defense when a project has not performed as expected. Compare now (1) "Jack provided a rationale for his conduct" and (2) "Jack offered a rationalization for his conduct." Sentence (1) indicates that Jack, as justification for his conduct, gave a reasoned, consistent, objective, and, in general, fair and unprejudiced account explaining why he did what he did; (2) implies that by way of justifying his conduct, Jack allowed himself to use, if not actual falsehoods, at least exaggeration, omission, distortion, and whatever other means might serve to overcome dubiety and skepticism.

rear/raise: the rule is that one rears children and raises crops. The verb *raise* is a causative verb, based on *rise*, and thus means "to cause to rise." Whereas such a background meaning may be sufficient to describe the process of tending tobacco, fruit, or vegetables, it would seem to be inadequate as a description for tending children, in the caring for whose growth more than food and water are necessary; children need to be trained, need to be taught, and need to be loved. Using *rear* to describe bringing them up at least separates the process in children from the comparable but not similar process in the case of plants and vegetables; the possibility of inferring such a difference in the use of *rear* recommends its use.

rebate/refund: both words signify the return of money (or other commodity) that was paid in making a purchase of some product or service. The meanings differ, however, in that a rebate is a partial repayment, whereas a refund is repayment of the total purchase price. Rebates figure in certain sales promotions where, on the mailing in of coupons or product labels, the customer receives a return of part of the purchase price; other promotions promise refunds ("your money back") if the purchaser is dissatisfied with the product.

recount/relate: both words mean "to tell, to give an account of," but *recount* adds the semantic component "in detail." One could therefore give as the meaning of *recount* "to relate in detail." Thus, instead of saying "He related in detail what had taken place in the previous week," one need only say "He recounted what had taken place in the previous week." And of course, to say "He recounted in detail . . ." would be redundant.

redolent/reek: both words refer to the giving off of odors, but *redolent* (an adjective) is customarily used of pleasant odors, *reek* (a verb) of odors that are sensorily unpleasing. Also to be noted is that *redolent* patterns with the preposition *of*, whereas the preposition that patterns with *reek* is usually *with*. Illustrative sentences: (1) "The garden was redolent of floral fragrances" and (2) "The stables reeked with the usual barnyard odors."

refute/confute: *refute* means "to show to be false or illogical" and applies primarily to assertions or arguments; *confute* means "to prove wrong" and applies primarily to the person or agency making the assertion or the argument. One will refute an argument by showing that its premises are wrong, its facts inaccurate, or its conclusions illogically arrived at; one will confute an arguer by showing the person to be inconsistent, the reasoning to be sloppy, confused, or incoherent. The difference in meaning resolves itself largely into a difference in focus—either on that which was said or on the person who did the saying. Having made an argument, a person could say either "Refute that, if you can" or "Confute me, if you can."

regard/regards: among the several meanings of *regard* is that of "reference or relation." The following sentences illustrate the word's use in that sense: (1) "With regard to the question of your chances for promotion, I'm afraid I cannot be very encouraging" and (2) "I have nothing further to say in regard to your chances for promotion." (The selection of the prepositions *with* and *in* in sentences (1) and (2) seems well motivated; apparently their use correlates with the meanings "reference" and "relation," respectively.) Another sense of *regard* is that of "respect or affection." When the word is used in the plural, these meanings translate into the meaning "good wishes," and it is this sense that figures in the phrase "with best regards" or "my best regards," commonly used at the end of letters. It is a common mistake to mix up the two forms described here; thus, we see uses such as (3) "We've gotten a lot of inquiries with regards to the availability of our new product" or (4) "In regards to your last question, I have no good answer." The misuse illustrated in (3) and (4) probably results from the influence of another use of *regard*, namely, that in which it functions as a verb, with the meaning "to concern," as in a sentence like (5) "As regards the question you raise, I'm afraid I don't have a very good answer." In (5), *as regards* functions more or less synonymously with *in regard to*, so that, by contamination, the plural form is employed in the latter construction.

regretful/regrettable: a person is regretful, a situation may be regrettable. Therefore, there is a misattribution of regret when someone says (1) "No matter how regretful it is, we have to acknowledge that the system permits abuses." Whatever "it" is in this sentence, it is not a human being, and so, although it may have or feel regret, it cannot be regretful. By way of clarifying the latter distinction, consider that a group or organization can be said to regret something, but it apparently cannot be represented as being regretful about something; thus (2) "The administration (the court, the association, and so on) regrets that it cannot proceed with this project," but not (3) "The administration is regretful that it cannot proceed with this project." An expression like (3), however, is the sort that would appeal to speakers who think that by avoiding the proper but ordinary expression and employing instead an impersonal and longer form they are adding a bit of gloss to their language.

relation/relationship: a relation is any kind of connection or association between people or things; a relationship is a state or condition that results from a background of such connections or associations. A relationship is regarded as more significant than is a relation, which might be established on the basis of some temporary, contingent, or accidental fact or event; thus, two people might find themselves in some sort of relation with each other on the basis of a friend's marriage, a new job, or the results of a lottery drawing, but in none of these or in other such cases need a relationship develop. One is thrown into a relation, but one develops a relationship. And this development usually requires a period of common experience and the acceptance of mutually agreeable terms. A relation between two people might be that of employer and employee, thus a matter of formal association; the relationship between them might be one of mutual trust or distrust, thus a function of their joint experience. In other words, events may lead to relations, but decisions lead to relationships. Two children bear a relation to each other in respect of having the same parents; the relationship thereby established is that of being siblings. Two countries might be said to have good relations with each other; their leaders might enjoy a good relationship. As a rule, it is events that lead to relations, but decisions that lead to relationships.

relative clause: this is a construction at which a goodly number of rather significant grammatical considerations come into play. One distinguishes between restrictive and nonrestrictive (or descriptive) relative clauses. Restrictive clauses are those that limit or confine an antecedent's range of application (in this sentence, for example, the word *clauses* is antecedent to a clause that limits the application of clauses to just such as limit or confine the application of that antecedent); the clause "that limit or confine an antecedent's range of application" is thus a restrictive clause. The other type of relative clause is the nonrestrictive type, which functions not to limit or confine an antecedent's range of application but instead to provide some descriptive content as to the nature of that antecedent (in this sentence, for example, the word *clause* is antecedent to a clause that describes the type of modification to be effected on the antecedent to which the clause applies); the clause "which functions . . . to provide some descriptive content . . ." is thus a nonrestrictive clause. After this bit of metalinguistic byplay, we may turn our attention to some important correlations concerning these two types of relative clause.

With restrictive clauses, the relative pronoun employed is generally *that*, although *which* is becoming more and more tolerable. With nonrestrictive clauses, however, *that* is impermissible, and *which* (or *who*, and so on) must be used. Another very important correlation involves punctuation. With restrictive clauses no comma should be used to separate the clause and its antecedent, whereas with nonrestrictive clauses the use of a comma is essential. Thus, compare (1) "Politicians who are corrupt should be sent to prison" and (2) "Politicians, who are corrupt, should be sent to prison." In (1) where, in the absence of punctuation, the relative clause is read as restrictive, the inference is that only some politicians should be sent to prison, namely, the restricted group that is corrupt; in (2) the relative clause is nonrestrictive; it describes politicians as a whole, the inference therefore being that all are corrupt and consequently that all should be sent to prison. In speech, different intonation patterns correlate systematically with these two types of clause (or should).

It is not only in relation to the relative clause that the comma may play its role as an indicator of whether a syntactic segment is or is not to be construed as restrictive. Consider the following message recently displayed on a TV screen as an advertisement by a mutual fund—let us call it the Banana Fund: "The Banana Fund. Outperformed all mutual funds with more than twice as much average return." The intended meaning was that the Banana Fund produced more than twice the average return for its investors, and thus outperformed all other mutual funds. This reading would have been accomplished by inserting a comma after the word "funds." As the sentence stands, however—that is, in the absence of a comma—its meaning is that the Banana Fund outperformed all those mutual funds that produced more than twice as much average return as it did—a rank contradiction. The correct reading requires that the prepositional phrase (beginning with the word "with") function nonrestrictively. But the improper punctuation causes that phrase to be read as restricting the preceding noun phrase "mutual funds," producing a message that totally belies the Banana Fund's outstanding performance.

An interesting corollary of the difference between restrictive and nonrestrictive modification is reflected in certain constructions in which the modifier occurs not in a following clause but as a prenominal adjective. Thus, consider the sentence (1) "The workmen were ordered to repair the defective lintels." If the word "defective" were to occur in a following clause, would that clause be restrictive or nonrestrictive? This difference is neutralized when the modifier is preposed to the noun. Thus, it is not clear from (1) whether all the lintels are defective and need to be repaired or whether only some are defective and only those need to be repaired. Compare in this connection the frequently heard announcement "This offer is available at all participating stores," an announcement that leaves hanging the question of whether all or only some of the stores are participating in the offer. In an advertisement for a company promoting a new technique for treating breast cancer, there occurs the claim that the treatment involves "no harmful radiation." As it stands, the claim would permit radiation, so long as it was shown not to be harmful. The modifier, in other words, would be read as nonrestrictive, a reading permitted by the syntactic arrangement.

relevant/pertinent: both words mean "related to the matter at hand," but their meanings differ along the dimension of specificity or pointedness. *Relevant* means "worthy of raising in the context of discussion"; *pertinent* means "applicable to the point at issue." Thus, age might be a relevant consideration in evaluating a person's fitness for a job, but it would be a pertinent consideration only if a certain age were part of a job's specifications. The question of age would be "raiseable" (Lat. *relevare*, "to raise, lift up") in the context of a general discussion regarding an applicant's fitness, but the question would "pertain," that is, have pointed reference, to the prerequisite mentioned in the job's specifications.

reluctance/recalcitrance: reluctance is a feeling that is experienced; recalcitrance is an attitude that is shown. I can vouch for my reluctance, but I can only characterize someone else's recalcitrance. I can say "I am reluctant to comply with your demand," but I could not very well say "I am recalcitrant to comply with your demand," although someone else could say such a thing of me. A reluctant person is someone who is loath or unwilling to do something; a recalcitrant person is someone who is opposed to or unwilling to do something. Reluctance may be induced by a variety of factors; recalcitrance will usually be evoked by orders or commands.

repeatedly/repetitively: the following sentence was encountered in a recent publication: "For over two generations, wine loving consumers such as yourself have discovered our company and stayed as customers, repetitively reordering our wines over the years." In this quotation the word *repetitively* calls attention to itself, but probably not in the way that the writer of the sentence intended. The word normally to be expected in the context of the sentence would be *repeatedly*, the use of which would convey the intended impression. A repeated action is simply one that takes place over and over again; a repetitive action is also one that takes place over and over again, but it is one that, in so doing, tends to become boring, to displease by its sameness. It should be noted that the practice of bypassing the expected word and substituting for it a word that is less common can sometimes lead to happy results. But the practice must be governed by an awareness of semantic nuances. Simply to substitute a word that is less common in the context, longer, and more immediately impressive poses its dangers. People who indulge in this practice should be aware that such indulgences usually occasion a double take on the part of their readers and that the second take is not favorable to the author's gambit.

repellent/repulsive: *repulsive* describes a characteristic of a person (or object); *repellent* describes an impression projected by a person (or object). A person is repulsive; a person's behavior is repellent. In respect of this distinction, *repulsive* is like such adjectives as *cheerful, sensible, dutiful,* that is, such as describe types of character or personality, whereas *repellent* is similar to such adjectives as *forbidding, aggressive, demanding,* that is, such as describe conduct or manner. One reacts to a person as being repulsive, to a person's conduct as being repellent: Compare (1) "I had always found Tim to be affable and cooperative, but his behavior at that moment was repellent" and (2) "I had always found Tim to be cheerful and good-natured, but his manner at that moment was repulsive." In (1), *repellent* implicitly focuses attention on Tim's conduct (and implicitly on the effect that it produced on the speaker), whereas in (2), *repulsive* focuses it on Tim (and the speaker's reaction to Tim). An interesting use occurs in Jane Austen's *Sense and Sensibility*. Marianne writes a letter to Willoughby in which, after she describes the unaccountable reserve that he displayed toward her on the previous evening, she exclaims, "I was repulsed indeed!" where the meaning is that Willoughby had deliberately fended off her requests that he explain his, in the circumstances, inexcusable failure to reply to her letters. Austen has Marianne use *repulse* rather than *repel* so as to focus attention not on Willoughby's conduct during the encounter (in his evasions he is as polite as ever), but to focus it on him. It was not Willoughby's actions that put Marianne off; it was himself.

reply/response: both words refer to an answer or reaction of some kind, but *reply* is generally used when the answer is understood to be verbal—either written or oral; *response*, by contrast, has a more general application, that is, may be used for a variety of reactions: thus, "Her response to his request was a mere shrug of the shoulders." To describe a reaction of this sort, *reply* would be ill used. Compare (1) "John's account of the ordeal suffered by his family elicited no reply from his friend" and (2) "John's account of the ordeal suffered by his family elicited no response from his friend." Sentence (1) suggests that the account elicited nothing verbal but leaves open the possibility that some other reaction was manifested or might be forthcoming; sentence (2) suggests more a sense of totality; not merely was there no verbal reaction to the account, there was no reaction of any sort. In the circumstances, the failure to reply is perhaps understandable—the news might have rendered John's friend momentarily speechless; the failure to react at all, however, implied by the use of *response*, permits the inference that John's friend is unfeeling, lacking in sympathy.

reproof/rebuke: both nouns refer to an expression of criticism or disapproval, but *rebuke* has this meaning in a stronger sense; one may speak of a gentle reproof, meaning thereby an act of criticism perhaps motivated by a kindly or constructive purpose, but the meaning of *rebuke* would not likely tolerate such modification, being more compatible with modifiers like *harsh* or *stinging*.

resonate/resound: the following sentence was recently overheard: (1) "Today, we hear voices of hope resonating from churches throughout our area." Although to a large extent the meanings of our two words overlap (in fact, in most dictionaries each one is defined in terms of the other), there is at bottom a critical semantic difference, one that the context of (1) forces to our attention and that determines *resonate* to be the wrongly selected alternative. The semantic consideration relevant in the present connection is that *resonate* means "to expand, to intensify or amplify the sound of," whereas *resound* means "to throw back, to repeat, the sound of." Our sentence would therefore make better sense if it were recast as (2) "Today, we hear voices of hope resounding from churches throughout our area."

restless/restive: both words mean an unquietness, an activeness, but *restive* contains a semantic component of balkiness, of resistance to some control or regulation, so that whereas *restless* signifies a moving about, *restive* signifies a movement against. In both (1) "Alice was restless" and (2) "Alice was restive," Alice is being described as moving about or mentally agitated; in (2), however, there is implied a reaction to a constraining force.

revolt/rebel: both words mean "to renounce obedience to the law or dictates of a government or a ruler," but *rebel* adds the component "and attempt to overthrow the existing order." Refusing to adhere to certain laws would be a measure of revolt, whereas an armed uprising would be a rebellion and, thus, more than a revolt. To revolt is to refuse to obey the constraints imposed by another; to rebel is to attempt to replace those constraints by a set of one's own.

rhetorical question: an utterance having the grammatical form of a question but intended to function as a statement. A professor, having presented an analysis of a complex mathematical problem, instead of saying to the class, "That's the solution to this problem," might say, instead, "Isn't this an elegant solution?" In saying this, the professor does not expect to hear anything by way of response; the expected response is an implicit admission that the problem has been solved. In this particular case, the advantage of using a rhetorical question instead of an assertion is that the listeners, instead of being told the conclusion, are made to arrive at it themselves. In general, that is the function of rhetorical questions. They, as it were, smuggle in assertions without the speaker's needing to make them.

rite/ritual: a rite is an established form of religious or otherwise solemn practice; a ritual is a prescribed form for carrying out the ceremonies associated with such a practice. In the field of religion, a close connection obtains between the two: Thus, baptism in certain religions is a rite, the manner in which it is performed being a ritual. In Great Britain, because of the monarch's role as head of the Church of England, the crowning of the monarch constitutes a rite, one that is carried out with solemn and elaborate ritual. All rites have associated rituals, namely, the procedures whereby the rite is executed. But there are many ritualized procedures, practices that follow fixed and unbroken rules, that are not contingent upon rites. Thus, for some people it may be a ritual to put their right shoe on before their left, but this practice—although never deviated from—obviously has no religious or otherwise sacramental significance.

salubrious/salutary: the meaning of *salubrious* is narrow and precise: "promoting or beneficial to health"; that of *salutary* is more general: "conducive to some beneficial result." Thus, a salubrious effect might be produced by a change of climate, a new diet, a course of medical treatment, and the like, all things whose bearing is on the physical health of a person. The causes for a salutary effect, by contrast, are not so narrowly restricted. A good scolding, for example, although having no effect on the health of the individual concerned, might very well, in causing that individual to reflect on and modify conduct, have a salutary effect. Similarly, a visit to a counselor might have a salutary effect on the relationship between the partners in a marriage or between parents and their children—quite while leaving the (physical) health of those involved completely unaffected.

sanguine/sanguinary: the meanings of both words are based on that of an etymon (Lat. *sanguis*) referring to blood. *Sanguinary* more directly reflects this etymological origin in its meaning: "bloody, attended by bloodshed." *Sanguine* originally referred to one of the four humors (along with *bilious, atrabilious,* and *splenetic*), namely, that humor characterized by the prominent role that the blood played in that person's balance of bodily fluids and that manifested itself in a ruddy complexion, hence a healthy appearance, hence a cheerful disposition, hence a confident mien or character. Compare "Donald has a sanguine/sanguinary countenance." Either version would make sense, but the latter would be appropriate only if blood were actually visible to the onlooker. However, if one were speaking of dispositions of character, one could use the word *sanguine*, but *sanguinary* would be inappropriate.

sarcastic/sardonic: compare (1) "Whitey Hogg is a sarcastic person," (2) "Whitey Hogg is a sardonic person," (3) "Hogg made a few sarcastic remarks," and (4) "Hogg made a few sardonic remarks." Strictly (perhaps pedantically) speaking, (2) and (3) are proper expressions, (1) and (4) are not. The reason for this judgment is that sarcasm is a matter of speech, sardonicism a matter of personality or temperament. It might be worth observing that the uses (1) and (4) illustrate the type of metonymy based on the transfer of cause and effect. Thus, in (1) the effect (sarcasm) is attributed to the cause (the person), and in (4) the cause (the personality trait) is attributed to the effect (the speech). This type of transfer is very common in English; thus, we speak of scornful language, pompous language, timid language, and we speak of ironic, grandiloquent, and precise personalities. Although the background distinction concerning these words is worth pointing out, the usage that they exemplify is so firmly entrenched in English that it is probably an overreach to call it into question.

scare quotes: a specialized use of quotation marks to highlight or call attention to a word or phrase that is being used in an unusual way, so that I might write "Another function of quotation marks is in their use as 'scare' quotes." In this sentence the plain, unmarked use of *scare* would result in an unusual, a questionable, appearance. The use of the quotes around the word signals to the reader that the usage is indeed unusual, but that there is a reason for it; in this instance, we are made to reflect that the quotes are intended to scare us into *noticing* the word within the quotes. Compare the following sentences: "Whales are not really 'animals,'" spoken by someone who is pushing a theory that runs counter to the prevailing scientific view; further "If Windelband is a 'genius' (i.e., as oddly enough, he's been called), then standards must be changing."

seasonal/seasonable: *seasonal* means "pertaining to the seasons" or "periodical"; *seasonable* means "suitable to the season." Thus, *seasonal* refers to a characteristic of an event or phenomenon, whereas *seasonable* offers a judgment about that characteristic. We might therefore say either (1) "The falling of leaves is a seasonal phenomenon" or (2) "The falling of leaves is a seasonable phenomenon," with the difference that (1) implies that periodically, at the appropriate time, the falling of leaves takes place, whereas (2) implies that the occurrence of falling leaves is customary and expected. Additionally, there is about the use of *seasonable* an indexical quality, a quality that directs its use onto the extralinguistic context in which it is used, this quality being absent from the meaning of *seasonal*. Thus, we may say either (3) "Weather is seasonal" or (4) "This weather is seasonable." Exchanging our two words in these sentences would produce in each a result that would strike us as counterintuitive: To say (5) "This weather is seasonal" would be to express a banality, if not indeed a tautology ("This weather is not seasonal" being inherently contradictory), whereas to say (6) "Weather is seasonable" would be to make a highly dubious claim.

self-esteem: everywhere these days one hears of the need to develop a person's sense of self-esteem; one hears this particularly in pronouncements by teachers and members of the educational establishment, where one of the recommendations for certain programs is that they lead to a heightened sense of students' self-esteem. A former judge, in the course of deploring the treatment accorded to prisoners, stressed particularly the harmful effect that certain practices had on prisoners' sense of self-esteem. My objection to this usage is not to any efforts that would promote the development of people's opinion of themselves. But why refer to such efforts as means for the promotion of self-esteem? What happened to the old-fashioned notions of self-worth or self-respect? In this elevation from respecting oneself to esteeming oneself, we have another example of the manner in which the language is used to inflate a notion's significance; someone at some time had occasion to refer to the principle of self-respect and decided to raise its expression a notch on the semantic value scale. The psychologically grotesque result is that it is no longer sufficient to respect ourselves; we now find it necessary to hold ourselves in esteem.

sensible of/sensitive to: compare "I'm sensible of my shortcomings ... of your disapproval ... of the need to make amends" and

"I'm sensitive to your criticism . . . to loud noises . . . to the complaints of subscribers." *Sensible of* means "aware of"; it refers to the mental registration of some fact or condition. *Sensitive to* means "affected by, responsive to"; it refers to a mental state that will prompt a reaction to some fact or condition. Compare (1) "I am sensible of the needs of others" and (2) "I am sensitive to the needs of others." Sentence (1) indicates a recognition that others have needs; (2) indicates a recognition and responsiveness to those needs.

A note might be added here on the difference between the phrases *sensitive to* and *sensitized to*. Fundamentally, the difference consists in the fact that the former phrase refers to a state or condition, the latter to a process. Consistent with this difference is the fact that a person will be said to *be* sensitive but to have *become* or *been* sensitized. True, a person may also be said to have become sensitive (to something or other), but this will be the result of having undergone a process of sensitization.

sensuous/sensual: both words mean "appealing to the senses," but the meaning of *sensual* includes as well the semantic component "appealing to the appetites," where the appetite particularly in question is the appetite for sexual gratification. Therefore, where the feel of fine leather or cashmere might offer a sensuous pleasure to someone, that pleasure would be converted to a sensual gratification if the leather or cashmere enveloped a human body.

sexual/sexist: the distinction between the meanings of this pair is somewhat similar to that in the pair *racial/racist*, treated earlier. A sexual remark would be one that referred to sex; a sexist remark would be one that referred to a sex, usually invidiously or in an otherwise disparaging fashion. Thus, a woman could be a participant in a sexual act but be the object of a sexist remark (the same could be said of a man).

shambles: plural in form but singular in meaning, the noun *shambles* derives from a form that earlier meant a bench or table on which meat was cut up and displayed. It subsequently assumed the meaning of a place where food animals were slaughtered, that is, a site for butchering. It now refers generally to any place of carnage or widespread destruction. The usage consideration in connection with this word concerns not so much its meaning as the proper syntactic construction in which it should appear. One encounters usages such as (1) "When the rioters departed, the city's central district was (left) in shambles" or (2) "When the rioters departed, the city's central district was (left) in a shambles." In (1), the use of the preposition combines with *shambles* to form a descriptive phrase, on the order of "in chains" or "in agony." In (2), the prepositional phrase makes it appear that the city was (left) in some sort of receptacle or container. The usage that reflects the word's proper meaning would be (3) "When the rioters departed, the city's central district was (left) a shambles," that is, with no preposition. This usage makes it clear that *shambles* describes a certain kind of place. Compare "The rioters made (of) the city a shambles."

short-lived: with regard to this entry, the question is one of proper pronunciation. In pronouncing this word, the second element is properly pronounced with the vowel sound of *dive*, not that of *give*. The word is composed of the elements *short* and *life*, and means "having a short life," so that the underlying element is the noun *life*, not the verb *live*. And whether that element undergoes inflection, as in the plural *lives*, or derivation, as in the adjective *lively*, the vowel sound is the same as that in *life*. The word *long-lived* is not of such common occurrence, but the same considerations regarding pronunciation apply in its case as well. (Cf., further, *short-breathed*, where it is the noun *breath*, not the verb *breathe*, that figures in the composition and that, consequently, determines the pronunciation.)

sic: Latin for "thus, so" and used to indicate that a form or spelling that appears to be improper or incorrect is to be understood as representing what the writer intends. This can be made necessary when something is being cited or repeated and the form being represented was rendered incorrectly in the original; for example, citing from the account of a football game, one might represent a line in that account as follows: "According to the Alligators' coach, 'On fourth down the Terriers were forced to bunt [sic].'"

sign off on: a currently fashionable expression, apparently originating in Washington, D.C., which apparently means "to agree to, to join in on." For some obscure reason, this phrase is being used instead of a phrase like *sign on to*, which would convey in transparent terms what *sign off on* conveys in terms that are opaque. The difference between *transparency* and *opacity* in this context is the difference between expressions whose meaning is a function of the meanings of their constituent words and expressions whose meanings must be arrived at in some other way—through consideration of the contexts in which they are used, through logical inference, through explanation by paraphrase, and so forth. Since *sign off* means "to cease broadcasting (or transmitting)," it is not clear how *sign off on* is to be taken as meaning "agree to" or "join in on." As an example of a typical use, consider "Congress would be reluctant to sign off on a deal that would benefit only the very wealthy" or "Does this document have to be signed off on by anyone other than the directors of the company?" There is a certain perverseness about the expression; it is semantically unsuited for the role it is being asked to play. Like other such arbitrary usages, however, it is currently fashionable and thus will probably have to be put up with for a while.

significance/signification: it is only signs—such things as words, numerals, symbols, and so on, and things that can function as signs—traffic lights, semaphore flags, Morse code signals, and the like—that can have a signification. However, a wide variety of dissimilar things—a gesture, a facial expression, an unanswered letter—can have a significance. The signification of a sign is its meaning, what it signifies; the significance of a gesture is its import, what it signals. Both signification and significance are forms of communication. They differ in that signification communicates via means that are designed for communication, whereas significance can be communicated by means whose primary function is something else.

simple/simplistic: *simple* means "plain, uncomplicated"; *simplistic* means "characterized by a forced, an unwarranted simplicity." Thus, the following sequence encountered in a manual describing the manufacture of cigars might very well produce in one a quizzical reaction: "Question: How is a cigar constructed? Answer: Very simplistically." In general, a simple solution to a problem would be one that was uncomplicated but that nevertheless constituted a solution (it might in fact be a brilliant solution); a simplistic solution might also be uncomplicated, but it would be one that either overlooked dimensions of the problem or one that did not account accurately for certain complex aspects of it. It would neither inspire confidence in an idea nor confer credit on its propounder to hear someone say, "I have a simplistic idea that I think will take care of all your objections."

single/singular: in its most characteristic use, *singular* means "special, unusual." It is thus not a near-synonym of *single*. Of course, it does have the virtue of containing one more syllable than *single*. This fact and the phonetic similarity it bears to *single* provide a strong temptation for some speakers to use it instead of that word. Overheard recently was the following sentence: "We should not be asked to vote on a measure based on the singular effect it might have on race relations." This sentence might be appropriate if the speaker thought that the measure might have a specially significant (a singular) effect on race relations and objected to being asked to vote on the basis of only that criterion. But that was clearly not the intent of the speaker, whose objection was to being asked to cast a vote with an eye on the single criterion of the measure's effect on race relations.

six foot/feet tall: in expressions like "six-foot tall," "four-mile hike," "two-inch nail," and so on, the forms *foot, mile,* and *inch,* which appear to be singular forms where plurals are required, in fact are plurals. Their background as plurals has been obscured, however, by certain developments in the history of the English language; the forms, in fact, represent the normal phonological development of Old English genitive plural formations, namely, *fōta, mīla, ynce.* The genitive was the case normally used in this construction—the so-called genitive of measure. Originally, the phrases given here would have been construed as "six of feet tall," "four of miles hike," "two of inches nail." By regular phonological development, the final *-a,* the mark in Old English of the genitive plural with these nouns, was dropped, resulting in the current seemingly singular forms (*six-foot tall,* and so forth). Because the understanding of the plural significance of the nouns in these phrases has been lost, they have been reformulated, with *feet, miles, inches,* respectively.

solecism: a grammatical or lexical blunder, particularly if the blunder is striking. If someone should say "I have every expectancy of passing the bar exam this time," that expression, in its surprising and unwarranted substitution of *expectancy* for *expectation,* would constitute a solecism. More typically, solecisms occur as formations—lexical or grammatical—that have no place whatever in the language; thus, a form like *irregardless* is a solecism under any circumstances, as is a grammatical construction like "Less than five people in the world understand this problem." Similarly solecistic is the use of *like* in a sentence like the following: "I feel like I am giving them a lecture on good government."

solicitude/solicitousness: both words refer to a concern (or anxiety) for someone or about something, but a nuance of semantic difference may be claimed as between these two words on the basis that *solicitousness* refers to this concern in a more pragmatic, less abstract fashion; thus, whereas *solicitude* designates concern (or anxiety) as a trait, *solicitousness* suggests the *application* of that trait. Compare (1) "Harry's solicitude for his father's health led him to take a job closer to home" and (2) "Harry's solicitousness for his father took various forms: He bathed him, he fed him, and he spent hours talking to him." In (1), the solicitude (the concern) is directed toward the *health* of Harry's father, hence toward a condition; in (2) the solicitousness (the application) is directed toward Harry's father, a person. One can do something *about* a condition, but one does something *for* a person.

speak to: normally, one speaks to a person or to a group of persons—an assembly or convention, for example. Although it is not necessary that the targets of speaking be human, they must at least, it seems, be animate—so that we might speak to dogs or birds but not, in the ordinary course of events, to rocks or trees. Now, however, a voguish usage has sprung up in which one "speaks to" such things as problems, issues, conditions, and other abstract and lifeless entities, to wit: "Rose Sunstein spoke to the problem of the homeless in our cities," "I can't speak to that issue," and "I wish to speak to the condition of the railroads in our country." I am not sure how many people are put off by this usage, but to my ears it conveys a subtextual sense of self-congratulation, an intimation that those who so speak regard themselves as linguistically au courant and, as such, have adopted a more sophisticated means for the expression of their ideas than the customary means employing the words *address, discuss, raise, speak about*, and so on.

specialization/specialty: *specialization* refers to the process of becoming specialized; *specialty* refers to a special pursuit, occupation, or product. Compare (1) "Farnham's specialization is in foreign affairs" and (2) "Farnham's specialty (therein) is Latin America." Sentence (1) says that Farnham has become specialized in foreign affairs, but (2) says that he is special in dealing with the foreign affairs of Latin America. Compare now (3) "Farnham's specialization is foreign affairs" and (4) "Farnham's specialty is in Latin America." Both these sentences are syntactically ungainly. It appears that *specialization* requires construction with *in* (cf. 1), whereas *specialty* simply equates with the stated specialty (cf. 2). (It should perhaps be mentioned that British English prefers the form *speciality*, as opposed to American English *specialty*.)

specie/species: this article is occasioned by the headline to an article that appeared in a recent newspaper: The headline read "An Endangered Specie." At first glance, it appeared that an error had been made, but perusal of the article, which was about a European currency, showed that the author had made a clever play on the similarity between *species*, which means "a biological genus" or "class of individuals," and *specie*, which means "coin" or "coined money."

specificity/specification: *specificity* refers to a character of definiteness or explicitness in a description or account; *specification* refers to an item of definiteness in such a description. *Specificity* therefore has a more general reference than does *specification*, whose reference is narrower. Compare (1) "One of the commendable things about Russo's analysis is its specificity" and (2) "One of the objections to Russo's analysis was to its specification." Sentence (2) leaves the reader with a sense of incompleteness; since *specification* refers to a particular item, one expects that item to be specified, identified, as in "One of the objections to Russo's analysis was to its specification that a special surtax would have to be imposed."

specious/spurious: both words refer to something that is in fact false or inauthentic, despite its appearing genuine on the surface. The difference lies in the fact that with *spurious* the lack of authenticity lies in the character or nature of the thing in question, whereas with *specious*, the failure derives from willful or deliberate deception. A spurious argument, say, would be one that normal analysis would reveal as being false, illogical, or fallacious, whereas a specious argument would be one that by subterfuge or deception achieved an appearance of soundness, and thus required in order to disclose its illogicality an additional or more intensive analysis.

stalactite/stalagmite: both words refer to the icy deposits formed in caverns that result from the dripping of mineral-rich water. Those that hang down from the ceiling are the stalactites; those that form on the ground are the stalagmites. One way to remember which is which is by associating the *c* of *stalactite* with the ceiling and the *g* of *stalagmite* with the ground.

stet: the Latin for "let it stand." Used in the preparation of manuscripts for cases where a writer, having struck out a passage, decides on second thought to let the passage stand as originally written.

strangle/strangulate: both words have the meaning "to compress a duct or vessel so as to restrict the passage of something through it"; the difference is that *strangle* implies a focus on the result of this process, whereas *strangulate* focuses on the process itself. Thus, a strangled person has been choked to death by the (complete) cutting off of air from the windpipe, but referring to an organ or bodily canal as strangulated means that pressure is causing it to narrow or tighten. *Strangulate* lends itself more readily to metaphoric applications than does *strangle*; thus, ambition, hopes, desires may be said to become strangulated, but such abstractions would hardly be said to be strangled. The reason is that strangling requires an agent (or agency) for its carrying out, whereas strangulation requires no such agent; someone is strangled by someone, but something simply becomes strangulated. Thus, whereas reference to the strangling of hopes would require the naming of the strangling force, reference to the strangulation of hopes requires no such attribution. Compare (1) "The American embargo has strangulated the Cuban economy" and (2) "The American embargo has strangled the Cuban economy." Sentence (1) implies that the Cuban economy has become severely straitened, whereas (2) suggests that it has been totally destroyed.

stress: as a factor in a person's psychological development, the function of stress is usually to induce a depression of spirits; in linguistic matters, stress functions, rather, to effect a highlighting or elevation—a rendering prominent of certain words or syllables. And in performing this function it may produce significant semantic consequences. Thus, consider the sequence (1) "dancing girls." With the primary stress on *dancing*, the sequence is rendered a nominal compound, with the meaning "girls who are for dancing" or "girls whose profession it is to dance." With the stress on *girls*, however, we obtain a phrase with the meaning "girls who are dancing." Now consider the syntactically similar phrase (2) "dancing shoes." With the stress on *dancing*, the meaning is rendered as "shoes that are for dancing," that is, like the first reading for phrase (1). If the stress in this phrase is placed on *shoes*, however, the meaning yielded is that of "shoes that are dancing," a meaning that might refer to an activity in a fairy tale or in a ballerina's nightmare, but not one that would have any application in the normal course of events. In fact, if anyone were to say "I just bought a beautiful pair of dancing shoes" and stress primarily the word *shoes*, a listener would be justified in reacting, at least, with bemusement.

The differences in stress placement may have implications for the writing of these phrases. Thus, consider the title of a recent TV program: "Inside the Mind of a Child Killer." Was this intended to mean (a) "Inside the mind of a child who was a killer" or (b) "Inside the mind of a killer of children?" As it happened, the killer in question was a thirteen-year-old, so that the meaning intended was (a). The stress, thus, would have fallen on the first syllable of *killer*, and the rendering of the title is correct as it stands. But suppose that the program was about an adult who killed children? In that case, the stress would have fallen on *child*, and the resulting compound would need to be written *child-killer*, that is, hyphenated (the rules for hyphenation are not hard and fast, however, and it would probably not be necessary to hyphenate the comparable formations given here that involve the word *dancing*).

This determinative function of stress is to be distinguished from the role that stress plays in the speech of certain second-language speakers of English, in whose speech, because of stress patterns inculcated by their primary language, English words turn out to be stressed in some less than appropriate fashion. Thus, native speakers of Czech or Finnish will tend to stress words like *assistance, compatible,* and *forgive* on the first syllable, carrying over into English a rule to stress first syllables, a rule that is operative in their native language. Stress misplacements of this sort, however, have as a rule no potential for semantic differentiation; they impart to the speech of such speakers what is usually called an "accent," but the consequences of this sort of stress mismanagement are merely superficial; they are not, as is the case with the intrinsic English stress function, semantically critical. Consider, for example, what would be suggested about the country's long-standing capacity to assimilate new immigrants if, in saying "The United States is a melting pot," we were to place the stress on *pot* instead of on *melting*.

strong and weak verbs: verbs are called strong if there is a change in the stem vowel in moving through the principal parts of the verb—where it is this change in the vowel "grade" that signals the different grammatical functions, that is, present, past, past participle: thus, *ride, rode, ridden; sing, sang, sung; break, broke, broken; find, found, found,* and so on. Verbs are called weak, however, if the stem vowel is unchanged through the principal parts and where the feature that signals the different grammatical functions is the addition of a so-called dental suffix: thus, *cough, coughed, coughed; talk, talked, talked; rub, rubbed, rubbed; wait, waited, waited.* These two classes do not exhaust the types of verbs in the English language, but they are the two most fundamental.

submission/submittal: the verb *submit* may mean either "to yield to the power or authority of another" or "to present (something) for consideration." These two fundamental meanings of the verb stand to each other in somewhat of a passive-active relationship. Compare (1) "Hank usually submitted to his sister's tyrannical behavior" and (2) "That afternoon Hank submitted his resignation." In these uses no problem arises, inasmuch as what follows the verb makes clear the voice function (passive or active) of the verb. Nominalization of the verb, however, yields both *submission* and *submittal*, and here a minor problem arises. Even though dictionaries sanction the use of *submission* in sentences like (3) "Hank's submission of his resignation came as a surprise to everybody" (thus, irrespective of whether the submitting is of a passive or active nature), such a use sets up something of an interpretative shadow—did Hank bring his resignation under submission? This problem is easily circumvented simply by using the form *submittal* in all such cases, that is, where the voice function is active; thus, (4) "Hank's submittal of his resignation came as a surprise to everybody."

substantial/substantive: the meanings of the two words overlap to a considerable extent. The respect in which a distinction may be drawn is perhaps best conveyed by citing a context in which either word may occur and describing the different senses that result when one of these words replaces the other. Consider "The governor presented several _____ reasons for raising taxes." The use of *substantial* in this context would suggest that the reasons presented by the governor were weighty, of considerable importance; the use of *substantive* in this context would suggest that the reasons presented related to essential aspects of the problem, were thus of an undeniable significance, and, as a result, had a certain cogency. Substantial reasons might be prepossessing but not necessarily convincing; substantive reasons, by contrast, would have a fundamental relevance that could not be easily disregarded. It is mostly in the context of abstract notions like reasons, arguments, and so forth that either of the words may occur. In the context of nouns referring to physical objects, *substantial* would most likely be the proper term, as in "He built a substantial foundation for his house" (cf. "He built a substantive foundation for his conclusion.").

sullen/surly: both words indicate a dark mood and an unreadiness to speak, but *surly* adds to this general attitude a component of irritability and unreasonableness. Sullen people would put one off by their general attitude of gloom and dissatisfaction, surly people by the threat of displaying their bad temper.

sympathy/empathy: etymologically, the meaning of *sympathy* amounts to "a feeling with," that of *empathy* to "a feeling into." In their use, *sympathy* means the stimulation in a person of feelings that are similar in kind to those that affect another person; *empathy* means a mental or affective projection into the feelings or state of mind of another person. *Empathy* therefore allows for an appreciation of the feelings or state of mind of another person but not necessarily for a sharing in those feelings. However, sympathy (with another person's sorrow or joy) presupposes the presence of those feelings in the person having the sympathy. Compare (1) "Ellen sympathized with Arnold over the loss of his father" and (2) "Ellen empathized with Arnold over the loss of his father." Both sentences refer to Arnold and the death of his father, but (1) conveys the semantic shading that Ellen tried to imagine what it (the death of his father) felt like, (2) that she tried to imagine what he (Arnold) felt like. Recently, a person who had suffered such a bereavement said, "People can sympathize with me, but they can't empathize with me."

A note on the adjectival form of *empathy*: Should it be (1) *empathic* or (2) *empathetic*, both of which occur? (1) would seem to take for a model such forms as *psychopathic, homeopathic, neuropathic*, and the like, that is, forms in which the adjectival form is based on a compound, whereas (2) is formed on analogy with *sympathetic*, where the adjectival form is derived from an underlying noun. Given this background, it would seem that since *empathy* is, like *sympathy*, a noun, the preferred adjectival form should be *empathetic*.

synecdoche: a rhetorical figure whose major subtype consists in using the part for the whole: Common examples are use of *hands*, *hearts*, *bodies* to refer to people, use of *sails* to refer to ships, and *roofs* to refer to houses. Synecdoche is at play when a college student refers to a roommate as a "brain" or when a baseball manager refers to the "arms" he has in the bullpen. Other subtypes make use of the genus for the species (calling a dog "a beautiful animal," for example), use of the material for the thing ("my sheepskin" for the coat), use of a proper for a common noun (referring to a poet as "a Shakespeare"), and so on.

systemic/systematic: *systemic* means "deep-seated, integral, built into the system"; *systematic* means "periodic, occurring with regularity." Compare "Lying is systemic in political campaigning" (in other words, given political campaigning, there will be lying) and "There was systematic lying in the campaign conducted by my opponent" (lying occurred at regular, perhaps at predictable, intervals).

tactile/tactual: both words have meanings relating to touching and the sense of touch, and in some contexts there is not much to determine the use of one rather than the other of these two forms. One can distinguish between them, however, on the basis of the meaning "arising from or due to touch" for *tactual* and the meaning "capable of, allows for being touched" for *tactile*. In the following sentences, the respective uses of one or the other of our two forms is conditioned on these two meanings: thus, (1) "Football is an eminently tactual sport," (2) "Kissing is one of the more pleasurable tactual experiences," (3) "Among other things, cashmere is preferred to wool for its superior tactual properties," (4)

"Unlike the gases, oil is a tactile substance," and (5) "the coach's anger as he addressed the press was almost tactile."

talk/speak: in many contexts these two words may be used interchangeably with little or no difference of meaning resulting. In contexts like the following, however, substitution of one for the other of the two words would lend to each of the sentences a slight semantic jitter: (1) "Bill speaks well," (2) "Bill talks incessantly," (3) "Bill speaks a cultured variety of English," and (4) "Bill talks like a barroom bouncer." Comparing (1) "Bill speaks well" with (5) "Bill talks well," we infer from (1) that the reference is to the manner in which Bill says what he says, from (5) that it is to the substance of what he says. The distinction is that *talk* refers primarily to what is said, *speak* to the manner in which it is said. Compare the sentence (6) "Bill talks trash" with (7) "Bill speaks junk": Sentence (6) implies that there is a characteristic content in Bill's speech, a content that signals contempt or disrespect; (7) implies that there is a certain tendency in his speech, a tendency that defines his speech as of a certain type, namely, junk (cf. the introduction in this volume). An instance of (6) might be one basketball player saying to another "I'm gonna make you look like garbage tonight," of (7) might be a journalist writing "The police shot a man after they say he allegedly lunged at them," where the "allegedly" is totally redundant (given "they say") but is included for its smack of technicalese and (of course) for the extra phonetic baggage that it incorporates.

temporize/procrastinate: both words mean "to delay, defer, or put off," but whereas the putting off associated with procrastination is occasioned by mental uncertainty or psychological difficulties, conditions that render the subject incapable of action, the delay associated with temporization is accomplished by the performance of certain acts or by the engaging in some activity. Comparing the sentences (1) "When Mendy Snyder was asked for his decision, he temporized" and (2) "When Mendy Snyder was asked for his decision, he procrastinated," we infer from (1) that Snyder did something "at the present time" to put off the need to decide; he may have raised questions, rehearsed options, invited comments or, perhaps, simply asked for more time, whereas from (2) we draw the inference that Snyder withheld comment as he tried to overcome certain mental conflicts and come to a decision. In essence, the delay associated with temporization is accomplished by doing something, that occasioned by procrastination is accomplished by doing nothing.

tendency/inclination: both words mean something like "a disposition to behave in a certain way." The respect in which their meanings can be differentiated lies in whether the disposition is regarded as situated in the person's mind or character or whether it is regarded as manifesting itself in a certain type of behavior. Thus, compare (1) "Harris has a tendency to argue" and (2) "Harris has an inclination toward argument." (As variants, we have (3) "Harris tends to argue" and (4) "Harris inclines toward argument.") In (1) and (3), we assume that Harris has a predilection for arguing, is naturally prone to argue, that it is in his nature to do so; from (2) and (4), however, we assume that Harris's conduct orients itself toward, proceeds in the direction of, arguing. The semantic valence of *tendency*, we might say, reverts backward, toward the subject; that of *inclination* projects forward, toward the object. Consistent with the difference sketched here is the fact that *inclination* is used when the disposition is contingently exercised: Thus, one can say (5) "When I read that contemptible article, I had a strong inclination to write to the editor." In a context like that of (5), *tendency*, with its sense of general, standing disposition, could not be used. We say "I have a tendency to . . ." but "I had an inclination to . . . "

tense (and aspect): tense is a marker on verbs that specifies the time at which the action, process, or condition that the verb refers to is considered to take place. As the time continuum is segmented into three basic subdivisions—present, past, and future—there are those three fundamental (grammatical) tenses, as in "he works, he worked, he will work." Time can be further subdivided, however; thus it is possible to speak of the immediate present, the recent past, the near future, and so on. Every language has the means wherewith to refer to such gradations of time. In English we can say "I am at this moment finishing *War and Peace*," "I just finished *War and Peace*," and "I'm about to finish *War and Peace*." In these examples the refinements of tense are conveyed not by grammatical means but by lexical means, that is, "at this moment," "about to," and "just." Some languages have the means to specify these gradations of time built right into their grammatical systems; just as English uses an inflectional ending to indicate past tense and an auxiliary word to indicate future, these languages use similarly grammatical means to indicate times like immediate present, recent past, and near future.

In English, in addition to present, past, and future, we speak of perfect and imperfect tenses, as well. This practice, however, reflects an imprecise understanding of the notion of tense. Unlike descriptions like "recent past" and "near future," where the additional terms really modify the idea of time and so may be regarded as specifying variations on the fundamental tenses, in phrases like "present perfect" or "past imperfect" the additional words have nothing to do with time and should not be thought of as modifying the tense word; the additional words refer, instead, to an independent component. This component is aspect.

Aspect does not modify tense; rather, it characterizes the state or condition of the action (indicated by the verb) at the time at which the action takes place. Thus, "I have written a letter to John" (present perfect "tense") indicates that at the present time (the time of utterance), the act of writing a letter has been completed, perfect(ed). If we cast this sentence in the simple past ("I wrote a letter to John"), we can see that the aspectual modification has no bearing on the time of the action but bears rather on its character. In both sentences the action is seen as having taken place in the past, but the first version, in emphasizing the completed state of the action, lends to that action a relevance for the present that the second does not convey. As a reply to the question "Would you like to join me for lunch?" the response "I ate lunch," would, as not focusing on the immediate situation, be an unsatisfactory reply, leaving open as it does the question of just when in the past the person had eaten lunch and whether having eaten lunch at that time was relevant to the present time. This question would not arise were the reply to have been given in the proper aspectual form of either "I've eaten lunch" or "I've had lunch," replies that would make clear their relevance to the question that had been asked. (A senator, on being asked a question, replied, "As I already said . . ." In saying that, he left open the response, "When? Was what you then said relevant to the question I've just asked you?" [and notice the role played by "just" in making the response apply to the present moment].) In the same way, "I will have written a letter to John" (future perfect "tense") conveys a sense of relevance, in this case to some future time ("when I next see you"), that would not be conveyed by the simple future "I will write a letter to John." Finally, "I was writing a letter to John" (past imperfect or progressive "tense") indicates that at some time in the past the act of writing a letter to John was in progress, had not yet been completed, was imperfect(ed). Notice how in a sentence like "People I've spoken to yesterday assured me that the deal will go through" the presence of *yesterday* introduces a sense of temporal dissonance given the implication of present relevance suggested by *I've spoken*. The aspects to keep essentially in mind are the "perfective," indicating completion of the action represented by the verb, and "progressive" (sometimes "durative"), indicating the continuing nature of the action represented by the verb.

terminus/terminal: a terminus is simply the end or conclusion of something, but a terminal is a structure or installation erected at a terminus. A city might be the terminus of a railroad line; its station or its maintenance yards might be regarded as terminals.

terse/concise: when we wish to characterize brevity or succinctness of expression, we use *terse* to characterize this property in a person, *concise* to characterize it in a message. Compare the following sentences: (1) "Dorothy responded to the question with a terse answer" and (2) "Dorothy responded to the question with a concise answer." In (1), the focus is on Dorothy's manner of giving the answer; in (2), it is on the nature of the answer.

testament/testimonial: something like the following sentence was recently delivered by one of the nation's political representatives: "This agreement is a testament to the negotiating skills of our party's leader." This sentence embodies a common error, namely, the use of *testament* where the word *testimonial* is required. The speaker should have said "This agreement is a testimonial (or "This agreement bears testimony") to the negotiating skills of our party's leader." A testament is a document in which something is testified to, thus, a will, a covenant, a book of the Bible, and so on. A testimonial, however, is a written or spoken expression of regard for a person's services or accomplishments. Another example of the same mistake: "Their ability to find relatively well-paying jobs . . . in an increasingly tough job market is a testament to the city's continuing capacity to absorb newcomers." In this case, the testimonial is not to a person but to something more abstract.

through/throughout: *through* is used in reference to a movement or passage that proceeds linearly, *throughout* to a movement or passage that proceeds spatially. Ink will move both through and throughout a blotter, for example. The movement through describes the passage of ink from the front to the back of the blotter—to its penetration of the surface; the movement throughout describes the passage of the ink laterally along the blotter, that is, to its spread through the substance. Typically, it is things that scatter or seep that move throughout an area. Whereas a bullet will pass though a board, such things as stain will spread throughout it.

throw the baby out with the bath water: the original (and for some speakers still) proper form of this saying is "throw the baby out with the bath." The expression dates from a time when a bath was given in a tub or basin, when it would be the contents of that basin—that is, the water—that would be understood to be the bath (cf. "running a bath"), and when after the bathing had been completed, the water would be thrown out. In such circumstances, it would be quite possible to throw the baby out along with the bath. As the bathing function developed into a form composing the modern permanently installed fixtures— what we now call "bathtubs"—the phrase was unconsciously adapted to present-day conditions, wherein bathing receptacles could not be lifted, let alone thrown, and the product accompanying the hurled baby was transformed into "the bathwater." The process involves a modified form of folk etymology, one in which the words are common enough but where the meaning (of "bath") has become opaque and is consequently reformulated into a semantically more comfortable variant.

timid/timorous: both these words mean something like "characterized by fear or lack of self-confidence." The difference lies in their application: *Timid* is used of a person, of a person's character or disposition, *timorous* of a person's action or behavior. One would therefore speak of a person as timid, of something that the person does as timorous: Compare "Despite his feeling for her, John was too timid to propose marriage" and "Although John made a few timorous advances, he could not bring himself to propose marriage."

torturous/tortuous: both words derive from a participial form of the Latin infinitive *torquere*, meaning "to twist" and from which the central derivative is the word *torture*, which, as a noun, means "bodily pain or suffering inflicted for purposes of punishment." This punishment was apparently inflicted originally by instruments such as the rack, which stretched or twisted the limbs of the unfortunate victims. *Torturous* is then an adjective that describes the process that inflicts torture or one that produces the kind of pain or suffering that normally results from torture; a torturous ordeal, then, might be one that is actually undergone by someone in a torture chamber, or it might refer instead to any experience that caused repeated or consistent pain or suffering, a session on an operating table, say, or in a dentist's chair. *Tortuous* does not contain in its meaning the implication of pain or suffering; it does trade, however, on the notion of twisting, so that by a tortuous argument one means an argument that does not proceed logically but twists and turns as it progresses and whose lack of straightforward development makes it hard to follow.

toward/towards: *towards* is originally an inflected (genitive) form of the adjective *toward*, which in Old English (Anglo-Saxon) meant "facing, approaching." This practice of inflecting an adjective (or a noun) to form an adverbial was a fairly common practice in Old English; compare *inwards* (*inward*); *homewards*, that is, "facing or approaching home," (*homeward*); and, with a noun, "He works nights," that is, "of a night." Against this background, the preferred adverbial form (preferred over *toward*, which also now functions as an adverb) is *towards*: "The weather turned cooler towards evening."

The form *toward*, however, may function, in addition, as a preposition. Essentially, choice between the adverbial or the prepositional form depends on grammatical considerations. Consider a sentence like "He felt a change in his attitude toward her"; or "I sense in his tone an antipathy toward his father." In these sentences, since the phrase introduced by *toward* modifies a preceding noun, that phrase must be a prepositional phrase and hence a preposition is required to introduce that phrase. But *toward* may also be used following certain verbs (if they are regarded as not implying action), thus we have "Our policy during this period tilted toward Iraq." However, in a sentence like "I didn't like the way he was sidling towards the exit," the phrase "towards the exit," as modifying *was sidling*, is adverbial, and an adverb is required to introduce it. (The distinction is nicely illustrated in two lines of poetry, one from Hart Crane's *White Buildings*: "The seal's wide spindrift gaze toward paradise" and the other from William Butler Yeats's *The Second Coming*: "Slouching towards Bethlehem to be born.")

The residual adjectival meaning of *toward* may still be observed in a sentence like "He was rather a toward person," meaning compliant or docile; compare in this context *froward* and *wayward*. The pair *beside/besides,* preposition and adverb, respectively, may also be mentioned as figuring in the general development here discussed.

transcendent/transcendental: both words take their meanings from a relation that they bear to experience. Ideas are transcendent if they have no ground in, if they transcend the bounds of, experience; transcendent, therefore, would be ideas such as that of the soul, of eternity, of God; these are ideas that we can entertain but whose "objects" we cannot know. Transcendental concepts, however, although also transcendent in relation to the grounds of experience (i.e., to the impressions made on our senses), are not disunited from experience; they, in fact, are necessary components of experience. According to Immanuel Kant, categories like that of substance, cause, and relation are a priori (transcendental) concepts of the understanding; in the sense that all sensory impressions of phenomena must, in order to be transformed into knowledge, be subsumed under them, these concepts provide the very possibility of experience.

transliteration: the rendering of a word in a new alphabet (or other type of writing system). If a word is borrowed from one language by another and if the two languages have different alphabets or writing systems, then the transcription of that word in the borrowing language is a case of transliteration. Thus, words like *glasnost* from Russian, *aliyah* from Hebrew, or *intifada* from Arabic are, as represented in English, transliterations. All words borrowed from Greek (unless they have been previously assimilated by Latin and borrowed therefrom) are rendered transliteratively in English.

truncate/curtail: respective meanings: "shorten, cut short." Consider (1) "Harley decided to truncate his speech" and (2) "Harley decided to curtail his speech." From (1) we infer that the act of truncation took place during the composition of the speech, from (2) that the act of curtailment took place during the delivery of the speech.

turbid/turgid: in their primary meanings, *turbid* means "unclear or murky," these characteristics being defined chiefly in respect to liquids, whereas *turgid* means "swollen or distended," these characteristics defined chiefly in relation to physical bodies. One might therefore speak of a wine as being turbid, intending in this way to comment on its consistency, or describe a wound as "becoming turgid," adverting thereby to its spread or enlargement. In these, their primary applications, there is thus little chance of confusing the use of these two terms. It is, however, in the secondary applications of these words that care must be exercised. Thus, in making a negative comment about a piece of writing or a use of language, either of these terms may be used. However, though both words convey negative connotations, those connotations are not equivalent. As their primary meanings would suggest, when we speak of a turbid prose, let us say, we are criticizing its incoherence or its lack of clarity, whereas when we speak of a turgid prose we are criticizing its inflated and overreaching character.

uninterested/disinterested: *uninterested* means "having no interest in, being indifferent to"; *disinterested* means "having no *personal* interest or stake in," hence "being unbiased toward." An opinion or judgment offered by someone who was uninterested in the matter at hand would have little significance, as the person who offered it, being uninterested, would have taken little or no pains to study or evaluate the problem concerning which the opinion was offered; a disinterested opinion, by contrast, might be of considerable significance—if handed down by a judge or a referee, say—since such an opinion would imply a thorough and complete examination of the problem.

A word might here be added about the prefixes *un-* and *dis-*. Both prefixes effect negation, but they effect it in different ways; *un-* simply negates the meaning of the word that follows, but *dis-* reverses that meaning (cf. *disaffected, disenchanted*, and so on). Thus, with *uninterested,* interestedness is, as it were, denied at the outset; *disinterested,* however, suggests the *withdrawal* of an interest that may, in fact, earlier have existed. That is why *disinterested* means not a simple lack of interest, but a suspension of that interest in the service of objectivity.

unjustified/unjustifiable: significant here is the difference in temporal orientation correlated with these two forms. An unjustified act is one for whose justification no past event or development can be adduced; an unjustifiable act is one for whose justification no future event or development can be adduced. Compare (1) "Nothing justifies what you did; it's totally unjustified," that is, you cannot point to anything that has happened that would justify what you did, and (2) "Nothing can possibly justify what you did; it's totally unjustifiable," meaning that no matter what you might say about it, what you did cannot be justified.

unsatisfied/dissatisfied: *unsatisfied* implies that a wish, need, or expectation that previously existed has not been satisfied; *dissatisfied* implies no such prior existence, but simply registers a failure to be satisfied. Compare (1) "My hope that you would by now have made some progress is unsatisfied" and (2) "I'm dissatisfied with your rate of progress." It appears that it is persons who are dissatisfied, whereas abstract notions of one sort or another are unsatisfied. Sentences (1) and (2) would therefore not tolerate the exchange of our two words.

use/usage: in linguistic matters, the difference between *use* and *usage* consists primarily in the fact that the former has a specific, the latter a general sense. One can speak of good or bad, proper or improper usage, and the good or bad, proper or improper use of a particular word. We can say "That use of the word conforms to the rules of good usage" or "The proper use (not "usage") of that word is as an adjective." Given a sentence like "Rennie speaks like his mouth is full," one can say that using *like* as an adverbial conjunction is incorrect usage or that the occurrence of *like* in that sentence is an incorrect use. The word *use* may be used also in a general sense, however; compare "Axie's use of the language suggested an extensive background of reading the best books" and "Grace's use of the subjunctive bespoke a solid background in Latin studies." These uses (this type of use) make it clear that in a sentence like "In periods of drought, one should cut back on the usage of water," *usage* represents an inflated use and a reprehensible usage.

used to: because of a particular phonetic property that inheres in the phrase "used to," it becomes possible for speakers to, as it were, "get away with" a mistake in the use of this form, a mistake that is disclosed when they have occasion to write the phrase. Forming the background for this possibility is the fact that in the speech of most speakers there is no detectable phonetic difference between their pronunciations of "use to" and "used to." This is because *used* ends with a dental stop and *to* begins with a dental stop and as is typical in such cases, assimilation occurs, that is, the voiced *d* gives up its voicing and accommodates itself phonetically to the unvoiced *t*, the result sounding simply like a single *t*; effectively, therefore, the phrases *use to* and *used to* sound the same. (The same simplification to a single sound is produced in such phrases as "fast track," "waste time," and "lost tool.") Consider now the sentences (1) "I use to read a lot of fiction" and (2) "I used to read a lot of fiction." There is no phonetic difference in the respective pronunciations. Sentence (1), although its use can be rationalized, that is, as meaning simply "I am in the habit of reading fiction," is of course not idiomatic English and so will not frequently be encountered. But a sentence like (3) "Although I don't do so anymore, I did use to read a lot of fiction," in which the dental stop marking past tense is on the word *did*, is perfectly good English. One of two errors may therefore occur: A person may write (4) "I use to read a lot of fiction" or (5) "I did used to read a lot of fiction." In these written sentences, the phonetic cover that availed in speech is rendered inoperative, and the writer betrays having led a charmed life in daily conversations.

valuation/evaluation: the meanings of these two words can be differentiated on the basis that *valuation* means "an estimated value," whereas *evaluation* means "the estimating of a value." Thus, a valuation is an objective measure of something's worth, whereas an evaluation is a process of examination that results in the imposition of such a measure. Consider the following sentences: (1) "In Amy Harding's opinion, current valuation levels in the stock market are too high" and (2) "Amy Harding's evaluation of the market's prospects struck many observers as too optimistic." In (1), Harding is commenting on the price placed by the market on its constituent stocks, the total representing a value that she thinks is greater than what the stocks making up that market are really worth; in (2), Harding is offering an estimate, based on her personal opinion, of the market's future course. The valuation of (1) would be the result of analyzing essentially numerical criteria, the evaluation of (2) the result of considering a variety of factors and arriving at a personal opinion.

venal/venial: *venal* means "capable of being bought," where what is in question are the dispensations or privileges that stem from a person's official or political position. A venal person is one who engages in the sale of such dispensations or privileges. *Venial* means "minor, not significant"; a venial error is an error that is not serious. In a theological context, a venial sin is one that is pardonable (as opposed to a mortal sin).

visit/visitation: a visit is an instance of visiting; a visitation is an act of visiting. Thus, *visitation*, unlike *visit*, may carry the connotation of an unexpected or undesired occurrence. When the bill collector comes to call, for example, that would typically be a visitation, not a visit. Compare (1) "My last visit from Donald was very enjoyable" and (2) "The last visitation from Donald was totally unexpected." A visit being an instance of visiting, it can be shared by both the visitor and the visitee (cf. in (1) "My last visit from Donald . . ." or "My last visit with Donald . . . "). A visitation, by contrast, being an act, is not so much shared as it is experienced or undergone. Although we can say (3) "My last visitation from Donald was totally unexpected," we would not say (4) "My last visitation with Donald was totally enjoyable."

viz. an abbreviation of Latin *videlicet* "it is permitted (*licet*) to see (*vide*)," but meaning, in practice, "namely," it represents a convenient device for elaborating on a point that has been made. Its meaning differs from that of *e.g.,* an abbreviation of the Latin *exempli gratia,* "for the sake of example, by way of example," a device that introduces instances of a class or category that has been previously mentioned; compare (1) "Some states, *e.g.,* California, New Jersey, and Florida, have borders on the ocean," (2) "Some words, *e.g., admire, detest, hatred, revere,* are dissyllabic," and (3) "I would like to comment on some of my opponent's claims, *e.g.,* his claim that the rich should be taxed more, that excise taxes should be established on all luxury items, and that taxes should be indexed." In these sentences, examples are given of the previously mentioned categories of (1) states, (2) words, and (3) claims. The examples that are given, it should be observed, are not exhaustive; they provide only a sampling of the classes that they illustrate. As opposed to this function, *viz.* is used to introduce not exemplifications of a class or category but, rather, to introduce examples that illustrate a principle; moreover, the examples presented with its use are presumed to be exhaustive: thus, (4) "My opponent has made three major claims, *viz.,* that the rich should be taxed more, that excise taxes should be established on all luxury items, and that taxes should be indexed" and (5) "Among the projects that the city must undertake, there are some that require immediate implementation, *viz.*, the repair of the sewer system, the purification of the water supply, the overhaul of the transit system, and the revision of the tax structure."

wait/await: there are a number of subtle differences between the meanings of our two words, not all of which can be tracked down in a single article. One significant difference is that *wait* frequently contains in its meaning a suggestion of immediacy, of presentness, of imminent realization, a suggestion that is not included in the meaning of *await*. Thus, compare (1) "John waited for the committee's decision" and (2) "John awaited the committee's decision." A fair inference from (1) is that John was expecting the decision to be rendered shortly, was perhaps waiting for it in an anteroom (this sense is even more forcefully conveyed by the form "John was waiting for the committee's decision"), whereas that from (2) is that the decision is not expected immediately, that John has been waiting for some time, perhaps even at home. Compare now (3) "I'm waiting for a friend (a delivery, a taxi, a phone call)" and (4) "I await your answer (decision, reply, and so forth)." Here again the things waited for in (3) are expected momentarily, whereas those awaited in (4) are foreseen as materializing in some respectably distant future. In keeping with the distinction drawn here would appear to be the uses in the following sentences: (5) spoken by a courtier to his superior: "I await your answer, my lord," that is, "answer at your pleasure," and (6) by a foreman to a new employee: "I'm waiting for an answer, son," that is, "answer me right now."

was/were: something like the following sequence of sentences recently appeared in a local newspaper: (1) "Roy said, 'I'm selling my stock in X corporation.' I don't think he was serious. But if he were, he'd better think twice about it." Even though the use of *were* in this context is incorrect, it represents a usage that is frequently encountered. By way of bringing out the flaw in its construction, let us consider the following two sentences: (2)

"When Roy said that he was going to remarry, I did not think that he was serious. But if he was, I knew that I would have to counsel him" and (3) "When Roy said that he was going to remarry, I did not think that he was serious. But if he were, I knew that I would have to counsel him." Both sentence (2) and sentence (3) can be given readings so that each one is correct as it stands. This can be shown if we paraphrase the two sentences: (4) "When Roy said that he was going to remarry, I did not think that he was serious. But if he indeed was serious, it was clear that I would have to counsel him" and (5) "When Roy said that he was going to remarry, I did not think that he was serious. But if he in fact were going to remarry, it was clear that I would have to counsel him." In (2), the use of *was* requires us to refer its clause to the question of whether Roy was serious or not; the indicative is used because Roy's frame of mind— whichever it is—exists as a matter of fact. In (3), the use of *were* requires us to refer its clause to the question of whether Roy would or would not remarry; the subjunctive is used because, although Roy said that he was going to remarry, that contingency was not yet actual but existed only as a possible eventuality. Whenever the contingency exists only in the mind of the speaker—as a conception or a possibility—the subjunctive mood is called for. Going back now to sentence (1), it is clear that the writer of the sentence intended the "but" clause to refer not to whether Roy was or was not intending to sell his stock but rather to whether he was serious or not. Therefore, the proper form to have used was the indicative *was*.

Mistakes involving this usage are quite common. They seem to occur because speakers, being unsure of the syntactic distinction involved and afraid to appear uninformed on a fundamental matter of usage, overcompensate and throw *were*'s around. Some examples of this uninformed overcompensation: (1) "When asked if Coleman were on the verge of being traded, he said 'Not really,'" (2) "I wouldn't wish to presume that he were lying at the time," and (3) "I couldn't tell her whether he in fact were at home or not."

To throw some additional light on the problem, particularly as it applies to sentences like (1), (2), and (3), consider the following extracts, which appeared some time ago in a newspaper review: (4) "To read this biography [of Picasso], one would think the artist were simply 'a sadistic manipulator,' who worked out his destructive relationships with women in his paintings." In this sentence the *were* seems off-key, seems somehow to violate a deep-seated grammatical consideration. Apparently motivating use of the subjunctive in (4) is the reviewer's disagreement with the author's conclusion that Picasso was "a sadistic manipulator," so that the statement, being "contrary to fact," requires the subjunctive. This inference is strengthened when one reads in the very next sentence of the article the claim that (5) "To read this biography [of Jackson Pollock], one would think that the painter were simply the self-destructive product of a dysfunctional childhood, who managed to translate the proddings of his unconscious onto canvas." Here again, the reviewer seems to disagree with—to find contrary-to-fact—the biographer's claim that Pollock's paintings reflected a dysfunctional childhood. Overlooked by the writer of these sentences, however, is the fact that it is only in conditional clauses that contrary-to-factness warrants use of the subjunctive. The reviewer might therefore have written a sentence like the following, in which the subjunctive would be properly used: (6) "If Jackson Pollock were self-destructive, his paintings would have assumed a quite different character." In (6), the subjunctive in the conditional clause indicates the reviewer's disagreement with the authors' claim. In (4) and (5), however, the subjunctive is occurring in main clauses; in those clauses, what is being set out is not the reviewer's response to the author's standpoint, but that very standpoint, and from that standpoint, naturally, there is no contrary-to-factness; therefore the proper form in (4) and (5) should be *was*. (Both (4) and (5) suffer from other grammatical improprieties as well—they both have double subjects, for example—but this article is already long enough without taking up any additional matters.)

whether (or not): although commonly so (mis)understood, *whether or not* is not freely interchangeable with *whether*. The function of *whether* is to introduce a disjunction between two alternatives. When only one alternative is explicitly mentioned, then the negation of that alternative is implicitly signaled by *whether* (the segment *or not* being superfluous); consider "I asked Rick whether he had mailed the letter." Consider now a sentence in which two alternatives are mentioned: "The Congress debated whether the measure enacted by the cabinet-level panel was legitimate or a flagrant abuse of governmental process." In a sentence like this, where two disjuncts (*legitimate* and *a flagrant abuse*) are explicitly cited, addition of *or not* would be superfluous and would serve only to complicate the sense of the sentence—by implicitly multiplying the number of relevant alternatives. Very commonly, however, *whether or not* is used in sentences where only one alternative is mentioned, and in sentences of this type care must also be exercised. Frequently, one encounters a sentence like "I asked him whether or not he thought that the economy was improving" (or "I didn't know whether or not he thought that the economy was improving"). In usages of this sort, the addition of *or not* introduces a subtle sense of semantic (logical) distraction, in that whereas the negation is intended to apply in the *complement* of the verb *thought,* it appears, by its placement, to apply to *thought*, thus making the sense of the sentence be "I asked him whether he did or did not think that the economy was improving," when in fact the intended sense is "I asked him whether he thought that the economy was improving or was not improving." In other words, the sentence is meant to elicit a judgment about the direction of the economy, not an opinion about its prospects for improvement.

There is also an intimation in the cited construction that the *or not* has implications for the verb of the main clause, that is, *ask*, thus making it appear that the meaning of the sentence is that whether someone did or did not think that the economy was improving, I asked him about it; in other words, regardless of what he thought about the economy's direction, I put the question to him. Compare the version "I will ask him whether or not he thinks that the economy is improving," where this sense is even more strongly suggested, namely, "Whether or not he thinks that the economy is improving, I will ask him about it."

The underlying consideration is that in sentences of this kind *whether* tacitly contains *in itself* the negative alternative, so that to express the intended sense, one could say (redundantly) "I asked him whether he thought that the economy was improving or not." Or one could simply say "I asked him whether he thought that the economy was improving," and the tacitly contained negative would be implicitly supplied after *improving*. But the tendency to pad out one's utterance is strong, so strong that I have heard a construction like the following: "This outfit can handle any sort of problem, whether or not it is a neurosis, whether or not it is a fantasy, or whether or not it is an illusion." Here the simple correlative *whether . . . or* construction has been distended with three superfluous and linguistically astonishing *or not*'s. Even more astonishing were the two following usages: "When I heard the voice from the next room, I didn't know whether or not it was the voice of my sister or whether or not it was the voice of my wife" and "He was unable to tell me whether or not he would attend the next day's meeting or not."

The phrase is used properly as a way to introduce a disjunctive condition, as in "Whether or not you agree with me, you'll have to admit that my argument is not without some merit" or "Whether you agree with me or not . . . " (I find, in fact, that I have found its use motivated in one or two other contexts, but I am not prepared to specify what those contexts are.)

whether/if: these words are frequently used to introduce indirect questions (a) or to indicate doubt or indefiniteness (b): thus, (a) "I asked him whether/if he had seen the latest report" and (b) "I'm not sure whether/if the mail has arrived yet." Only *whether* should be authorized in these constructions. Of relevance in this connection is the fact that among the functions of *if* is that of introducing a conditional clause, namely, "I'll accept your offer if you include a stable for my horse." This sense of conditionality is carried over when *if* is used in the constructions in question. Therefore, in a sentence like "I'm not sure if the mail has arrived," there is a slight intimation that the uncertainty is conditional on the mail's having arrived; that is, if the mail has arrived, then I'm unsure; this is an unwanted consequence and one that is avoided with the use of *whether*. Further, when clauses like "I don't know" or "It's not clear" begin a sentence, there is suggested a selection between two alternatives, that is, an either-or choice is implied. The word *whether* (which correlates with *or not*) conveys this sense of alternativity, and is thus, on these grounds as well, to be preferred in this construction, namely, "I don't know whether this is the correct solution to the problem (or not)."

willy-nilly: Consider the sentence "Harry Blitman will sign this contract willy-nilly," meaning that Blitman will sign the contract whether he wishes to or not. This curious formation goes back to a practice in Old English according to which the negative particle *ne* when it immediately preceded certain verbs would contract with those verbs to form a fused structure, so that from *ne will* was derived *nill*. The same contractive process took place between verbs and certain personal pronouns. In the present case, from *will he* would be derived, with some further phonological simplification, *willy*. Combining these two contractive processes, we get *nilly*. The construction before all these phonological developments took place would be "Harry Blitman will sign this contract will he ne will he," that is, whether he will or will not.

who's/whose: I would not have thought it should be necessary to write this article except that I have just seen printed on the television screen the question "Who's plan works?" *Who's* is the contraction of *who is*; the possessive form of *who* is *whose*.

whom: this article concerns a particular use of *whom*, one that is encountered with a fair degree of frequency and that is grammatically incorrect. Consider the sentence "The police arrested three varsity players, whom the coach said represented the heart of his offense." In a construction of this sort, the phrase "the coach said" should be regarded as a parenthetical insert and should be implicitly thought of as flanked by commas. When this is done, it suggests that the proper (i.e., the underlying) form of the sentence is "The police arrested three varsity players who, the coach said, represented the heart of the team's offense." This form makes it clear (the parenthetical nature of "the coach said" having been recognized) that the grammatical status of the relative pronoun in its clause is that of subject, not object; in other words, we have a (discontinuous) relative clause "who . . . represented the heart of the team's offense" modifying the antecedent "players." Following is another example of this error: "The killer was a homosexual gigolo whom friends say was worried about aging, and . . . "

It would probably not be amiss to take up here the more typical mistake involving this form, the case, that is, where *who* is used when *whom* is the form required. Consider the following passage, which appeared in a recent magazine article: "There's hardly a moment when you forget who you're watching." The required form here, of course, is *whom*. That form, however, is engaged in a struggle for its survival. Unlike the impersonal relative pronouns *which* and *that*, which assume the same form whether they occur in nominative or accusative function, the personal relative pronoun has a separate form as an accusative. Because of this systemic background, however, *whom* receives no implicit reinforcement from its associated forms and is thus specially liable to falling into disuse.

Index